MISTER ROGERS' PLAYBOOK:

INSIGHTS AND ACTIVITIES
FOR PARENTS AND CHILDREN

Berkley Books by Fred Rogers and Barry Head

MISTER ROGERS TALKS WITH PARENTS

MISTER ROGERS' PLAYBOOK:
Insights and Activities for Parents and Children

MISTER ROGERS' PLAYBOOK

INSIGHTS AND ACTIVITIES
FOR PARENTS AND CHILDREN

Fred Rogers
and Barry Head

Illustrations by Jamie Adams

BERKLEY BOOKS, NEW YORK

The recipe for Spaghetti Marco Polo from *From Julia Child's Kitchen* by Julia Child, copyright © 1975 by Julia Child. Reprinted by permission of Alfred A. Knopf, Inc.

MISTER ROGERS' PLAYBOOK: INSIGHTS AND ACTIVITIES FOR PARENTS AND CHILDREN

A Berkley Book/published by arrangement with Family Communications, Inc.

PRINTING HISTORY
Berkley trade paperback edition/April 1986

Cover photograph by Walt Seng.

ISBN: 0-425-08745-X

A BERKLEY BOOK® TM 757,375
The name "Berkley" and the stylized "B" with design are trademarks belonging to Berkley Publishing Corporation.
PRINTED IN THE UNITED STATES OF AMERICA

ACKNOWLEDGMENTS

We'd like to acknowledge the immeasurable debt we owe to Dr. Margaret McFarland who, with such wisdom and generosity, continues to guide our work for children and families. It was she who first gave us the understanding of the importance of play, and her lifetime of experience is reflected, directly and indirectly, throughout this book.

To Cathy Cohen Droz, of Family Communications, goes our sincere appreciation for her constant coordination as these words and pictures came together. Jamie Adams, our illustrator, also deserves a big "thank you," for his skill, sensitivity, and perseverance.

We'd like also to thank Elaine Lynch and Margaret Fuller of Family Communications for all their hours of work in the preparation of the manuscript. Their patience and persistence have been invaluable. To Gareth Esersky, our gratitude for believing the work was worthwhile and for her thoughtful and helpful editorial suggestions.

Finally, our heartfelt thanks to the many playful adults and children who, over the years, have shared their ideas and experiences with us—in particular, Richard Trost, auto mechanic *extraordinaire*.

For
Jim and John,
Tim and Andrew:
May they find ever-expanding playgrounds
of the mind, body and spirit.

CONTENTS

CHAPTER 1

PLAY: WHAT IT'S ABOUT

There's something about play that makes it very hard to define. It seems to be easier to say what play isn't than to say what it is. It isn't drudgery, for instance. It isn't something we're forced to do. A mother may tell her children, "Go outside and play!" and really mean it, but the kind of play the children choose is up to them.

When they come back at suppertime, she may ask, "So, what did you do all afternoon?" And when they say, "Oh, nothing," they usually mean they were playing. Nothing important? Nothing they care to talk about? Nothing they think a grown-up would be able to understand? Perhaps . . . and much more.

There's no doubt that children's play and grown-ups' play are different, and it may well be that as we grow older, most of us lose touch with what children's play is all about. It's hard to imagine most of us spending an afternoon doing "nothing." We might spend the afternoon playing, but that play would probably have a name such as golf, bowling or bingo. It would probably have rules and a purpose, and competition might be an important part of it. We might take it very seriously. We might even return from our play in a bad mood because we "played badly."

There's even something sinister about the phrase, "playing for keeps." That kind of play doesn't sound like fun to us. It might be dangerous, with some possibly bad consequences.

It seems to me that this change in play takes place quite early in life, perhaps somewhere about five or six years old. It has something to do with coming to understand about rules and outcomes and winners. It has something to do with believing that being loved somehow depends on being the "best" player. Some children never learn otherwise, and it's not surprising: so much of the adult play that they see around them or on television is deadly serious business with reputations and livelihoods depending on who wins.

The joy that older children and adults find in play may depend a good deal on what their earliest play was like—the play they engaged in before that time of structured competition began in their lives. How much had they found out about themselves and their place in the world? How much had they found out about love and anger and their relationships with others? How much had they come to feel that curiosity and creativity were valued by the people they loved? How much had *they* come to feel valued?

Those are the sorts of things that children's earliest play is about. Through their play they discover the world . . . and themselves.

Experts might disagree about when play begins, but that's only to be expected when experts might disagree about what play is. I don't think we can claim that a brand-new newborn is playing as it cries and wiggles and nurses and wets. To play, I think you have to do something intentionally—not much, perhaps, but at least something. I'm not sure we could say that month-old babies are playing when they kick their heels on a table to make a repeated sound, or when they watch their own fists floating in front of their faces, or even when they bring their fists to their mouths to chomp on them. Soon after, perhaps: that's when some babies learn to get more sucking pleasure by trilling their tongues against the nipple or bottle. It's also about then that infants learn to *stop* their hands as they float in front of their eyes. I suspect, though, that most of children's very first play comes not from some urge within them but rather in response to something the mother (or other close caregiver) does. If that's so, then a baby's earliest experiences of play are closely bound up with his or her earliest experiences of love.

When babies start responding to peek-a-boo, they may look solemn when their mothers cover their faces . . . and then, when their mothers uncover them, break into a smile and kick and bat their hands about as if to say, "Again, again!" We have no hesitation in calling this play. The baby is a participant, reacting each time in a way that makes the "game" continue.

That's the way I think it goes in those early days: the mother creates the play and invites the baby to participate. If you watch mothers and babies together, you'll see many, many instances of this kind of play. It might take the form of clapping the baby's hands together, accompanied, perhaps, with a rhythmic chant, or it might be a game of "This little piggie . . ." or it might be a bouncing-on-the-knee game.

Babies are, in fact, learning a lot through these games, but it certainly is play. They are learning where parts of their bodies are located and what it feels like when people touch them. They are learning how to give pleasure by smiling and moving in certain ways that make Mother laugh and continue hugging and playing. Although the thoughts and words certainly aren't there, there is an *experience* occurring that tells the baby, "I can make someone happy."

Doesn't that experience have to be a cornerstone in the development of healthy self-esteem?

In these games, babies play with their mothers' bodies almost as much as the other way around. In doing so, they learn what happens when they pull Mother's hair too hard or squeeze her nose too fiercely. They learn, from the "map" of their mothers' faces, how to read displeasure as well as pleasure. They learn to curb their more aggressive actions in favor of the things that clearly evoke delight.

Doesn't that have to be a cornerstone in the development of healthy self-control?

It isn't just mothers who play. Of course not. Dads play and so do brothers and sisters. Each plays in his or her own way. Their faces and expressions are different. The feel of their hands is different. Their degree of roughness and gentleness is different. They even smell different. And the members of the immediate family are probably just the most frequent players in the baby's life. After all, there may be uncles and aunts and grandparents, and there will certainly be family friends who coo and touch and stimulate in their own individual ways. Again, the words aren't there, the words that would exclaim, "They're all different!" But the experience of those differences is there, and it's leading to a readiness for a child to realize with amazement and, it's to be hoped, with pleasure, "*I'm* different, too!"

Imitation begins during these early months, and that introduces a new element into play. A baby may start copying Mother's mouth movements, clucking sounds or hand movements. Copying may become a game in itself, bringing reactions of delight from loved caregivers. The copied actions may then become part of the baby's play in the crib or playpen when he or she is alone.

By the time imitation happens, you can be sure that older brothers and sisters will decide that their new baby *can* play after all (finally!), and so play within the family is likely to gather new momentum. And all this time, babies, as they copy those around them or try out new things of their own, are discovering both what they have in common with you and me . . . and how they are unique individuals as well.

We see that as another cornerstone—a cornerstone of self-concept.

Play provides a foundation for so many things that are important to us throughout life. Self-expression is certainly one of those, and I associate it very closely with creativity. Finding ways to express who I am has been—and still is—a significant part of the work I do.

People sometimes say to me, "It must be great to write music and make television programs like you do, Fred. I envy creative people, but I just don't happen to be one of them." When people say things like that, it often turns out that what they're really saying is that they wish they were creative *artists.* Well, not everyone can express himself or herself as a creative artist, but that's only one part of being creative. I believe that everyone is creative because I believe that creativity is part of being human. Some forms of it are more visible than others, that's true. A huge abstract painting on a gallery wall, for instance, is certainly more visible than a research experiment in a laboratory, but it may not be more "creative." Being a composer may sound like a more creative kind of work than being the manager of a fast-food restaurant, but after a conversation with Stefano Galliucci the other day, I'm not so sure.

Stefano is twenty-four now, and we've known him and his family for a long time. There's Rena and Victor, Stefano's parents; a younger brother, Victor Jr., who's twenty-two; and two younger sisters—Rita, eighteen, and fourteen-year-old Becky. It's been particularly interesting to watch these children grow because play was always a big part of life in the Galliucci family. The four children have grown to be very different from one another in their interests and pursuits, but they all seem to share a lively curiosity and an excitement about trying new things. Although Becky is the only one who shows interest in becoming a creative *artist* (a painter), each is certainly creative in his or her own way.

Stefano has been working in the restaurant business for five years and has just become one of the youngest managers in a large chain of fast-food restaurants. As we talked, he told me what life was like in his "shop" (as he called his restaurant), and it became clear to me that every single day he was finding solutions, and often ingenious ones, to problems of product and presentation, maintenance, delivery schedules, inventory, employee management and training, human relations . . . and, of course, profit margin. Stefano is, in fact, leading a very creative life indeed!

I'm not sure how to define creativity any more than I'm sure how to define play. I feel fairly sure, though, that creativity has to do with rearranging known pieces into new forms. And it has to do with problem-solving. Rearranging and solving . . . those are two important aspects of play as well. It's not surprising because play, almost always, is a direct expression of creativity.

When I watch children play, I get particular pleasure out of seeing them use what they have to play with in unexpected ways. When they are very young, this seems to be their natural way to play because they haven't yet learned—or perhaps been taught— that certain things are meant for certain kinds of play. Doughnut-shaped disks of different sizes may be meant for stacking, in order of size, on a wooden pole; and a tin cup may be meant for drinking. But a toddler may discover, with delight, that a disk can fit in the cup, or that the cup can make a hat for a doll, or that the wooden pole can fit through the handle of the cup.

Parents, quite naturally, are pleased when their children begin understanding how things are meant to be used and when they start using them that way. I believe, though, that we need to keep encouraging our children to go on finding other than the intended ways to use things. In the ability to do so lies a lifelong capacity for discovery and problem-solving.

I remember Rena Galliucci telling me about a problem she was having one holiday season with her daughter, Rita, who was then a fifteen-month-old toddler. Rena had just finished decorating a small Christmas tree in the living room, and Rita couldn't keep her hands off its shiny ornaments and garlands. Scolding didn't help, and every time Rena put little Rita in her playpen, Rita would set up such a howl and hullabaloo that Rena would take her out again. Of course Rita would then head right back to the tree.

Rena's sister-in-law, Martha Warninski, happened to drop by. When she saw what was going on, she said, "Hey, Rena, instead of putting Rita in the playpen, why don't you try putting the *tree* in the playpen?" That did the trick.

Martha's suggestion, certainly, had to do with putting familiar things together in a different way, and it certainly was problem-solving, too. To me, it was also a solution that came from a playful mind.

ABOUT THIS BOOK

As I think of the material in this book, it occurs to me that a great deal of it has to do with the identification of things—whether they be feelings or shapes, how things are the same and people are the same and yet how they are different, what things are real and what are pretend, parts of the body, and everything else.

There's great value for children in learning to identify things and their uses, but that value goes beyond simply learning the right answers. Each time a child learns how something works or what it can do, he or she is gaining a little more understanding and mastery . . . more tools to *create* with.

We can be proud when our children learn to say "glove" and

to put gloves on their hands, or to say "shoe" and put shoes on their feet. But we can be proud, too, when they turn gloves into puppets and shoes into dump trucks!

You'll find many suggestions in this book for things to do with your children. In that sense, it's an activity book. But we hope it's more than that, too. We hope it will bring you some insights into play—why children play as they do, and why play is such an important part of their growing and becoming.

We'd also like to think that through this book you might find a renewed capacity to play in your own life. By that we don't mean just the orderly kinds of play that grown-ups are used to, but also "silly" kinds of play in which children find such delight. It may mean overcoming some inhibitions, and that's seldom easy. But there can be such rewards in relearning to be childlike in the true sense of the word.

If we were fortunate, much of our early childhood was a time of hope and laughter, a time of feeling loved, a time when all things seemed possible. Playing with our children can bring those times alive again.

And if our childhoods were times of sadness and hardship, playing with our children can help us come to terms with the feelings that linger with us from the difficult moments in our past. We may even find through children's play new feelings of optimism, a renewed sense that despite the pains we all experience as we continue to live and grow, the effort is worthwhile.

When a friend of ours learned that we were writing a book for families that would have activities in it, she said: "You know, we have lots of activity books at home, and I often run into a problem. I'll say, 'Hey, how about making something with play dough,' or, 'We could try to make an airplane if you'd like,' and what I'll get is sort of a shrug and a qualified 'Okay.' If I'm lucky, my kids will end up getting interested in whatever it is we've decided to do. As often as not, though, the activity kind of peters out half way through, and I can tell they really want to be doing something else. I find it hard to get their interest to begin with, and harder to keep it all the way through. Why is that?"

That's not an easy question to answer, and there's certainly no sure-fire recipe for getting a child to take interest in a certain activity at a certain time. It can help to remind ourselves that play is the outward expression of inner feelings, and the more we can encourage play about those feelings, the more willing to play a child is likely to be. It's not always possible, of course, because there are many times when we can't know what's going on in our children's heads.

Throughout this book, though, we've tried to suggest some of the feelings that preoccupy most children in their early years, and frequently we can see them confirmed in the play that children think up for themselves—play, for instance, about biting, or separation, or being in control. Talking about those feelings first can often provide a natural way to lead into making something that can be used to play about them.

Although almost all children confront many of the same tasks as they find out who they are and what their world is about, each child faces a unique series of circumstances and life events. Some of them will be stressful—such as moving, being hospitalized, or the death of a pet. During hard times, parents can help their children cope by encouraging play about them—before and after they occur. Play can ease the uncertainty and apprehension that may precede an event, and it can also help resolve the anger and sadness that may follow one. Being attentive to what is happening in our children's lives is another way to match activities with inner feelings.

Then there's children's natural curiosity about why things happen and how things work. When a child asks why a leaf floats instead of falls, or how a boat moves through water, we have a ready-made chance to suggest making a parachute or a paddle-wheeler. We won't always be able to find an activity in a book to match, but often we'll be able to adapt one or make up one to encourage this inner need to *know*.

For most children, one of the strongest inner urges is to be part of what their loved and loving grown-ups do. Children may enthusiastically participate in such "activities" as mopping, sponging, polishing, kneading, stirring or laundry sorting. These may seem like chores to us, but children are likely to see them quite differently—as a chance to help. That suggests that one of the best ways for us to engage our children in play is to play ourselves. I can easily imagine a scene like this:

A father sits at the kitchen table, quietly starting to make a milk-carton house. His four-year-old daughter is in the next room, watching television, but during a commercial, she wanders in to see what's going on.

"What are you doing, Dad?" she asks.

"Oh," he says, "I thought I'd see if I could make a toy house."

"Why?"

"Just for fun."

His daughter thinks about that for a moment. "Can I help?"

"Sure!" says her father. "I'd like that. I could use some help, too."

Half an hour goes by. Little by little the father has helped his daughter do as much of the project as she's able to do. When it's done, she picks up the house and runs upstairs to her mother.

"Look, Mommy!" she cries. "Look what Dad and I just made!"

One thing's for sure: it rarely works to impose a play activity on a child—just as controlling and directing our children's play rarely results in a happy and healthy play experience. The best we can do is to support and encourage play through example and gentle participation. Most of all, we can try to stay responsive to the inner urgencies of that remarkable and mysterious time called *childhood.*

As we play with our children, we are of course likely to grow closer to them in understanding. I know of no better way for a parent to recapture the feelings that went along with being a little child, feelings that for most of us now belong to a time we can't remember. As we experience those feelings once more through our children, we can begin to see the world a little more as they see it and as it once seemed to us. The chances are that such rediscovery can make us more responsive to our children in the ways we need to be.

A further word about the Galliucci family whom you have already met in this chapter: it seems only fair to confess that in fact they're imaginary friends of ours. We have used Rena and Victor and their children as a way to recount anecdotes from many people and situations in an informal and light-hearted form. They've served another purpose, too: as we've worked our way through the writing of this book, they've helped to keep *us* feeling playful.

CHAPTER 2

ACTIVITIES: THE EARLY DAYS

As we take care of *anything* that grows, we find out that different stages of growth bring different needs. Those changing needs are sometimes very clear—for instance, the need for different foods, or kinds of exercise, or ways of caring for the body. Other kinds of changing needs are not so clear, though. That's particularly true of ways of responding to feelings and, from a child's point of view, ways of expressing feelings through play.

We've already suggested that for children, play is a real need, and that an important part of taking good care of children is both permitting and encouraging that play. We may not be sure what kind of play children need at different times in their growth, but fortunately children have a way of letting us know by selecting the kinds of play that are important to them at the moment. We may sometimes find it hard to tolerate the kinds of play that our children choose. They may be intent on banging on pots and pans with a wooden spoon, or making messes with their food, or dropping things from their high chair again and again (and expecting them to be picked up again and again!). These forms of play may really try our patience, and parents' feelings are certainly every bit as important as the feelings of their children.

In the heat of a moment when our tempers are frayed, it's easy to scold, or shout, or even slap a hand. But however we show our disapproval, it's unlikely that a toddler, certainly, will understand the message that we're trying to send. What we're probably trying to say is "Don't make a mess!" What comes across to a toddler is probably more like "Stop trying to express your feelings!" That's a message that few of us would purposely try to send to our children.

Even when we're exasperated we may be able to pause long enough to remind ourselves of three things. The first is to set the immediate limits we need to set in a firm but loving way. Whatever we say or do, we should try to keep a clear distinction between disapproval of, say, banging on pots and pans right now, and disapproval of the *need* to bang on pots and pans at all.

The second reminder that we might give ourselves is that whatever our child is doing, it is coming from something he or she is feeling . . . and that feelings do need to be expressed. We may not feel so angry at what our child is doing if, even as we're stopping our child doing it, we're noting what it is and telling ourselves that it seems important for our child to do.

The third reminder is that we should look for a time and a place where those of our children's needs that we've noted *can* be acted out in ways that don't upset us. There's probably a time during the day when a lot of banging doesn't matter to us. That would be a good moment to put some pots and pans and wooden spoons out on the living-room rug or in the playpen for our children to play with. We might make time (just before bath time) and a place (on newspaper, a plastic sheet or the back porch) for healthy messing with finger paint, modeling dough or mud. We might take time out from our chores for a few minutes to sit beside the high chair and willingly retrieve the spoons or toys that our child throws down again and again—to make a joyful game together out of what otherwise could be an irritation.

No one can tell just when a child needs to engage in a certain kind of play, but young children's play does tend to move through predictable phases that take commonly shared forms of expression. You might find it interesting to watch for some of these patterns in your child's play, and so we thought we'd mention a few of the more ordinary ones here . . . and suggest some activities that could give your child acceptable outlets for his or her pressing inner urges.

Ins & Outs

One- and two-year-olds tend to be very interested in the insides and outsides of things.

HOLDALLS   At this age, these are likely to be popular toys: an old purse, a shoe, a glove, a box, a bag, a basket, a tin cup, or anything else that can hold things. Mouths, of course, hold things, too, and you may find that your toddler shows a lot of interest in your mouth. They're generally very interested in what their own mouths can hold as well, and that raises one of the constant cautions of early childhood play: *watch carefully when your child is playing with anything that's small enough to swallow!*

Sizes

As pre-toddlers and toddlers begin to understand that they are physically separate from the grown-ups around them, they often become intent on the difference between large and small.

BIG & LITTLE   You may find that your toddler likes to play with a big teddy bear and a small one, big dolls and little dolls, big shoes and little shoes, big balls and little balls. Many children have a toy that consists of a set of different-size wooden or plastic disks with holes in them. They're meant to fit over a spindle on a platform to make a pyramid shape. But like so much of toddlers' play, they may not be at all interested in what the disks are meant to do. Instead, they may spend a lot of time just playing with big disks and little disks in their own ways. What they seem to be asking in their play, over and over again, is "What does it mean to be small? What does it mean to be big? How do big and small things go together? And how do big and small *people* go together?"

Part & Counterpart

After a while, toddlers seem to extend this play about big and small to include things that are entirely different but nonetheless appear to go together in some way that needs to be understood. This kind of play may be a child's way of answering a new question, something like: "I'm starting to feel different than you, but we do belong together . . . don't we?"

BELONGING   You might want to include some objects in your child's play that do have ways of going together—not that they have to, only that they can. Even if you weren't to do so, though, your child would almost certainly make such "toys" out of everyday things. A lid goes with a pot. A spoon goes with a bowl. A shoe goes with a foot. And yes, a disk with a hole in it goes with a spindle. But—and here children show the spontaneous creativity that many of us seem to lose later on—a spoon can go with a shoe in certain ways (it might be a person in a boat), just as a disk can go with a bowl (it might be a cookie in a dish).

This exploration of part and counterpart has come to seem to me one of the truly significant breakthroughs of early childhood. Breakthrough may not be quite the right word, because it suggests a suddenness rather than a progression of growth. As it occurs, though, it initiates the lifelong process of seeking counterparts to ourselves—counterparts in our friends, in our spouses, and in our search for work that provides a satisfying counterpart to our hopes, our needs and our feelings about who we are and who we can become.

Messes

Messiness is another characteristic of toddlerhood. In fact, it's an almost universal one. At that age, children can't be expected to do much more with their arms and hands than make large movements, so on one level messing and smearing reflect the limits of a toddler's physical coordination. But that the *urge* to smear things around should be so strong and common in toddlerhood suggests that there's something else at work, that toddlers *need* to engage in this kind of activity. If that's so, then parents might find it helpful to provide outlets that satisfy their toddlers while still staying within the limits of parental tolerance.

MAKING MESSES   Toddlers are keen observers, and they often like to try to do the things that they see you doing. Your toddler may have seen you wiping up a messy table or sponging the kitchen floor. A pan of water, along with a sponge or a cloth, may turn out to be a very popular toy for your child and an acceptable one for you. You will probably have to set firm limits on where the water can be smeared around and where it can't, but that's all a healthy part of helping our children learn to channel their urges into appropriate forms of expression and where to start and where to stop. What's important is that we do provide outlets for them rather than trying to stifle altogether their urge to express themselves.

Finger painting on shiny shelf paper can be another outlet. You can buy commercial finger paint, or you can make a gooey mixture of soap flakes, water and a few drops of vegetable dye.

You can be sure that there will be plenty of the mixture that won't end up on the paper, but it will all clean up with water.

Homemade modeling dough offers another chance for harmless messing. The recipe is

> 2 cups flour
>
> 1 cup salt
>
> 1 cup water
>
> 1 teaspoon salad oil (optional)

> Combine all ingredients. The creations made of the mixture harden in about five or six hours.

Real dough—cookie dough—works well, too. In fact, it has one big advantage: you can bake the results of the mess and eat them later on.

Outdoor mud play with water is another alternative. That's a chance for a *real* mess!

Many parents become understandably upset when their toddlers get their hands into their own body products—their bowel movements—and begin messing and smearing with that. And it's true that the messing phase of children often begins about the same time as their curiosity about their bodies and their strivings toward toilet training. In fact, how parents deal with the one can sometimes affect the outcomes of the other. Once again, the important thing is to recognize the healthy urge of this age to make messes and then provide the materials that we feel are appropriate to make messes with. Then our children can begin to find satisfaction in learning to control and master their messiness.

Biting

The urge to bite is also common to toddlerhood . . . and a toddler's bite can hurt. Even at that age the jaw muscles are very strong. A bite may seem like a sudden, hostile, aggressive act, but that's not likely to be so. Biting can *develop* into an aggressive way to express anger, that's true, but at first it's often just a way to find out what a mouth with new teeth can do.

In fact, understanding what the mouth can do is a preoccupation that starts in early infancy. At that time, the mouth is the major source of pleasure, contentment, fulfillment, and other good sensations that add up to the feeling of being loved. Back then, the mouth can suck and "mouth" whatever comes its way. A little later, it can be more active and purposeful. It can chomp, and by then an infant's hands can bring it things to chomp on—to explore.

Teething changes things. To begin with, teeth hurt when they are coming in and cause a lot of unhappiness that even the most loving parents can't relieve. The chances are that a teething infant is feeling a good deal of what we've come to call misery, frustration, and anger. If babies with teeth are still breast-feeding, it's not unlikely that they will have tried out their teeth on their mothers' nipples—and have received a sharp reaction of displeasure in return. For some babies, that bite has even meant a sudden weaning to a bottle.

Life with teeth must seem much more complicated than it was without them! It certainly presents new and difficult challenges: finding out what's okay to bite and what isn't, and learning to control the biting urge itself. As with all challenges of early childhood, play offers the best place to face them.

MOUTHS   You may find your toddler is very interested in things that open and shut on hinges—things that are mouthlike. Opening and closing kitchen cupboard doors can become an irresistible pastime. Playing with the seat of the toilet can be another. Once again you'll find yourself setting limits for safety, convenience and appropriateness. As you do so, though, it will be helpful to make sure your child has other acceptable outlets for this kind of play.

For instance, you may have some small boxes with hinged lids around the house. (Bakery boxes are often made like that.) If not, you may have cardboard boxes with detachable tops. You can cut off one of the flaps that fit down over the bottom of the box and then tape that side of the top to the box's bottom to make the hinge. The stronger tape you use, the better. That silver-colored duct tape you can get in most hardware stores may be the best of all.

You might be able to find three or four boxes that fit one inside the other—and even paint them different colors. That way,

you'd have a simple toy that could help your child go on exploring big and little, inside and out, as well as the workings of the mouth. The boxes could be used as blocks, too—just setting one on top of the other.

Some toys have real mouths—animal toys and the like. They may even have mouths that open and close. Puppets' mouths often do so (*see page 97*). There's a time when toys with active mouths may become a frequent part of your child's play, but you may find that there's also a time when they seem too frightening for your child to play with. We need to respect fears like that and try to understand that they are likely to be the outward signs of some inner concern.

I certainly don't believe in forcing our children through their fears. I know there are some parents who think that by playfully menacing their children with a harmless toy they will help them learn that the toy is just that—harmless. But these parents may be missing an important point: *It's not the toy itself that the child fears.* What the child is afraid of is some inner feeling that the toy represents. A biting toy, for instance, might make a child fearful of his or her own urge to bite, an urge that he or she does not as yet feel able to control.

And if that urge *did* get out of control? Well, you might hurt someone you loved, and that person might stop loving you. For a young child, that can be a very scary thought indeed!

In fact, I don't believe it's healthy for young children's play ever to get frightening for them. One of the things we need to help our children learn is that play is a safe place to work on their feelings or to learn about the world around them.

Parents can help greatly in creating this sense of safety for their children. They can give their children safe places to play and safe toys to play with. They can help their children learn the difference between real and pretend. They can let their children know that their play is their own, to make of it what they will. And they can assure their children that they never have to push their play beyond the comfortable limits of their own inner readiness.

What *can* children bite? At first they can bite teething rings and hard rubber toys. Later they can bite hard, crunchy foods such as celery stalks and carrot sticks and biscuits. When children are encouraged to do that kind of biting, they're also learning something about healthy snacking.

Separation

Toddlers may also need to play with their feelings about your being away from them. Separation is a big concern of early childhood, and how we work on it then can have a lot to do with how we cope with times away from loved ones when we're much, much older. What young children need to know is that when the people they love go away, they also can come back.

BEING APART   If you have some little cars and trucks around, you could try some play with your toddler about going away and coming back. For a while, a larger truck and a smaller car might move around together. Then the truck might move away a little . . . and then come back. Or move away quite a bit, even out of sight for a moment or two . . . and then come back to the little car.

You can find out what your toddler wants to make the car and the truck do, too.

You can encourage the same kinds of play with human figures: adults and little children. (If you haven't any, you can make simple ones by cutting out pictures from magazines, mounting them on cardboard and sticking them in stands of bakers' clay.) When the mommy or daddy figure goes away, is there another grown-up who comes to stay with the baby? It will certainly be reassuring to your child to know that in real life that's always what will happen!

Some of the forms of play that develop between you and your child may turn out to be ones your child uses for comfort when

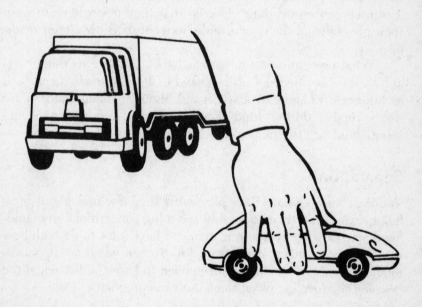

you really do go away. It's not unusual for children to get angrily upset as soon as it becomes clear that their parents are leaving—and to stay upset until their parents are out of sight. Once their parents are gone, they may then become subdued, thoughtful, or quietly sad as they work on accepting their parents' absence and the presence of their replacement caregiver. While they do so, they might go to Mom's or Dad's favorite chair (perhaps where they're used to being read to), and settle into it as though it were a parent's lap. Or they might head for the kitchen and recreate some play they're used to doing with their mom or dad. Or they might take up some of their toys and invent their own kinds of play about going away and coming back.

Soon, they'll probably be ready for new kinds of play with their baby-sitter.

That's not the way it always goes, of course. Your child will have his or her own ways of learning to cope with being without you. You might find it interesting, though, to ask your baby-sitters to note what happens after you leave, and to note it in some detail. That way, you can often get clues about how your child is coming to handle these earliest of life's separations.

Identity

As children move out of toddlerhood, their play moves with them and reflects their new interests and concerns. For the next few years, the big puzzle that children are likely to be working on is the "Who Am I?" puzzle . . . and it's a puzzle with a lot of pieces! Part of it is learning what it means to be separate and independent. Part of it is figuring out the relationships between that separate self and Mom and Dad and other people in the family and beyond. And another part of it is trying to understand how "me" is like other people and how "me" is different, and what those similarities and differences mean.

PUZZLES   This is a good time to encourage play with simple puzzles. They're easy to make. All you need is some cardboard to cut up into big shapes that fit together. You can paint the cardboard however you want to, or you could cover it—before you cut it—with a scrap of wallpaper or wrapping paper.

SORTING   At this time, sorting games make good toys, too. How about you and your child starting a "Jumble Box" full of things you usually throw away? You might start saving box tops and bottle tops, corks, toilet-tissue tubes, caps from empty toothpaste tubes and cans of shaving soap, empty boxes that razor blades come in, vitamin and medicine bottles, old dental-floss containers, perfume and cosmetic containers, spice tins and bottles, small boxes that foodstuffs come in, old spoons, old socks (you can stuff the feet with rags and tie a knot at the ankle), old shoe laces . . . and on and on and on.

If you feel like it, you can wrap bands of different colored tape around each of the objects you save. If you do so, you'll be able to encourage your child to sort all these things according to color as well as to size, shape, texture, use, and other ways you may think of.

(Your Jumble Box may have many things in it that a young child might want to put in his or her mouth—and might be able to swallow. You'll want to be sure to keep the box out of reach whenever you're not around to play with it, too.)

When Rita Galliucci was three and four, her mother tells us, she liked to play "wedding" with her play figures. At first, it seems the little girl figure was always the bride and the daddy figure was the groom. And the mother figure? Well, for quite a while Rita decided that the proper place for her was on the sidelines, watching, with a tiny baby in her lap. After a time, though, this wedding play changed so that the mommy and the daddy were the ones getting married . . . and the little children became attendants. That was one way Rita found to work on family relationships.

When he was about five, Victor Jr. was preoccupied by a set of toy tools his Aunt Martha had given him for Christmas. "He seemed to be able to play with them all alone for hours," Rena says. "He'd 'fix' anything that he could get his hands on. He wanted to be just like his dad. For a time he had another favorite kind of play, too. He'd take a big car and a little car and make them race around a table top. More often than not, the big car would end up crashing and the little car would win. I didn't think about it then, but looking back now I wonder if he wasn't working on his feelings about living with big people who seemed to have

all the power . . . and maybe about living with a very competitive older brother, too."

You'll see all kinds of play as you watch your children growing and trying to understand who they are and what they can do. Some of it may take us aback. There will be times when their play is clearly an expression of curiosity about who's a boy and who's a girl. Other play may seem destructive or aggressive—for instance, wrecking block buildings, scribbling all over pictures they've made, treating their dolls and animals roughly, or trying out words like "hate" and "beat him up."

We all have aggressive feelings—some of them healthy and some of them not. One task of growing is to learn the difference between the two. Another is to become able to express those that are *not* healthy in nonviolent, nondestructive ways. Encouraging our children's play, expanding its outlets as well as setting its limits, is one of the best ways we can help our children confront those tasks and grow to make constructive choices in other areas of their lives.

Some Other Ideas

CONTAINERS   We all seem to accumulate collections of odds and ends that need places for safekeeping. Children, particularly, tend to be avid collectors—of buttons, pennies, marbles, pebbles, or whatever. You can make useful containers out of a variety of empty food packages, and cuplike ones seem to work especially well. In fact, paper cups themselves are a good place to begin, and you can move up in size to margarine tubs and even to the tubs that pints and quarts of ice cream come in.

These kinds of containers are easy to decorate by covering the outsides with a thin coat of glue and then sticking on scraps of tissue paper, construction paper, or bits of ribbon and material. Another way to give them a character of your own is to put glue on the outside and then wind a length of yarn around and around until the whole container is covered.

Here's a construction-paper basket you could make together: First, fold one of the top corners of your sheet over to the opposite side so that the edges of the paper align. Cut off the piece below the folded part and save it. When you unfold the folded part, you should have a square.

Now, fold the square in half either way, crease it, and then do the same in the other direction. These creases will leave the outlines of four squares. But you need sixteen squares . . . so fold each side of the paper into the middle line, one side at a time, opening each fold-and-crease after you've made it. When you've done all four sides, you should be able to see the outlines of sixteen small squares.

This next part is like making a cardboard suitcase (*see page 151*). You cut one side of the corner square to your right—the side nearest you. Then turn the paper clockwise and do the same thing ... and again and again. All four corner squares should have one cut side.

The outside rows of squares become the sides of the basket. As you fold them up, you'll find that the squares you've cut make flaps that can fold around the corners of the basket. They'll need tape or glue to hold them in place.

Now, take the piece of paper you cut off at the beginning and fold it into a long, thin strip. That's the basket's handle, and you can tape it on or glue it.

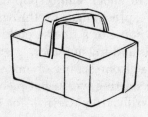

Making containers is an easy project and can be fun. You may find, too, that when you've taken the time to help your child make and decorate them, he or she is more likely to *use* them.

SCENT BALLS   You can make fragrant air fresheners by poking a dozen or so cloves into an orange and letting the orange dry in the sun or near a radiator for three or four days. The more cloves you choose to use, the stronger the scent will be.

If you want to hang the scent ball in a closet, or if you just want to make it look prettier, you might want to tie a piece of ribbon around the orange first, knotting it tight and then knotting the leftover ends once more to make a loop. You'll find that the small ends of the cloves are sharp enough to pierce the ribbon, and they can hold it in place.

Besides being pleasant to use here and there in your home, these scent balls make fine gifts for relatives and friends.

BEAN BAGS Bean bags are good for lots of different games. They can be used for catch, for seeing who can toss them into a hat or wastepaper basket, for trying to knock empty pop cans off a porch railing. A child can safely express anger by throwing bean bags at a blank wall, the side of a house or a tree. A child can also use them as small pillows for dolls and toy animals.

Bean bags are easy to make from scraps of material, old towels, shirts, and socks. If you're starting with a flat piece of material, you might want to make cardboard patterns—for instance, a cardboard square about 4″ on a side, and a cardboard circle about 4″ across. (Of course you can make the patterns any shape you want.) Your child might be able to help out in the beanbag-making by drawing around the patterns with a felt-tip pen, while you do the cutting out with scissors or pinking shears.

You'll need two same-size pieces of material for each bean bag. Once you've stitched the pieces together, almost but not quite all the way around, you can fill them with dried beans. Then all you have to do is finish the stitching. If you think you're going to use the bean bags for throwing games, you'll want to make the stitching good and solid!

GROWIES Watching simple growth take place can help children understand that growth takes time. More than that, though, they can learn that anything that grows needs nourishment and care.

Beans (the kidney-bean variety) are good sprouters. If you soak them overnight in water, they'll sprout faster. One way to "plant" them is to tuck them in between a ring of damp paper towel and the inside of a glass jar. With light and just enough water each day to keep the paper towel moist, the beans will soon begin to sprout. Once their growth is about two inches long, you can move them into paper cups full of soil. They'll still need light and water to go on growing.

A ½″ top of a carrot will do much the same thing. If your carrots have leaves, these leaves are likely to wilt, but new ones should sprout. If you start with leafless carrots, you'll need to put the tops in a shallow dish and add just enough water to cover them. They should sprout, too, and once they have, you can transplant them into soil.

You can start sweet potatoes growing in jars by immersing the bottom half (the pointed ends) in water. The potato doesn't want to rest on the bottom of the jar, so you may want to stick some toothpicks into the top half of the potato and rest them on the jar's rim. As the potatoes begin to grow, they should send roots out into the water and leaves out the top. After about two weeks, you can plant them in pots or, with warm weather, out in the ground.

If you'd like to try starting plants from seeds, half egg shells in egg cartons make fine starter pots when you fill them with soil. Once the plants are three or four inches high, you can put them in larger pots or in the ground, egg shells and all.

WITHOUT WORDS   We don't always need words to tell other people how we're feeling or what we want. Here are some questions for you and your child to think about . . . and act out if you feel like it:

- How does a dog tell you it wants to go for a walk?
- How does a cat say, "I like you?"
- How does a baby say, "I'm hungry?"
- How do people say *yes* or *no* without words?

Can you think up more than one answer? Here are some more:

- How could you say, "I love you," without words?
- How could you say, "I don't know?"
- When people wave "hello" and "good-bye," are the waves different? How can you tell which is which?

CHAPTER 3

THOUGHTS: PLAY & COPING

Mishaps, upsets, frights, accidents, and catastrophes—no one escapes them as we grow. Just as we have our individual ways of coping with them when they occur, so, too, do we have our ways of dealing with the feelings they leave with us when they are over. Most of us can remember a time that was very hard for us. It might be a time when we were painfully embarrassed, or a time of sudden illness or an operation, or it might be the death of someone we loved, or a terrifyingly near brush with death ourselves. How do we feel about that time now? How comfortable are we even thinking back to it?

It seems probable that every one of us has buried some painful events—and the feelings that went with them—so deeply that they're hard for us to find again. At the other extreme, some of us may still be so shaken by the aftershocks of a past event—even one long past—that we can't get any distance from it at all and can't seem to move beyond it. I think what we'd all like is for these crises, after a time, to blend into the landscape of our lives so that they no longer jump out at us when we look back at where we've been.

What makes the difference? There's no complete answer, but many of us who have worked with children have seen how helpful it is to them to talk and play about the feelings they have about the crises they've been through. It seems that children's strong feelings naturally tend to show up in their play, but it certainly helps if their close caregivers support such play by letting them know that it's not only okay but important. If we can learn to talk and play about our feelings when we're young, we may be able to take that capacity with us through life. It could make the difference, when strong winds hit us, between bending and breaking.

There are many kinds of childhood upsets. There are emotional and physical hurts; trips to emergency rooms; stays in hospitals; births of brothers and sisters; first trips to the doctor, dentist, or barber; going to school for the first time; moving to a new home; deaths of pets and people . . . the list could go on and on. There's one that I've mentioned before, and perhaps it's the most important one of all because it's a part of so many others: times when people you love leave you. There is so much that children can weather and weather well when someone they love is close by. And there are so many seemingly little things that can upset children profoundly when they're separated from those they love. You may be surprised to find how often, when your child goes through a crisis, there has been an element of separation involved. You may be surprised, too, to see how often your child plays about things that go away from each other . . . and then come back together again. That's one way children have of becoming more comfortable with the times when you have to be away from them—and of reassuring themselves that you will come back again.

This kind of play, of course, isn't only valuable in helping come to terms with things that have already happened. Many events that may cause anxiety are foreseeable. Play, in advance, can be such a help in feeling ready for them! Knowing so much more about what new experiences are going to be like, parents can be an important part of this kind of play by suggesting what's going to happen—and what's *not* going to happen.

Adults, it seems, are more likely to "replay" past events and rehearse new ones in their heads than with toys. We've all had the experience of reshaping past conversations or arguments so that they come out better for us than they did when they happened, or practicing for ones that are going to take place. I sometimes wonder whether it would be more helpful if we were still able to take toy figures and move them through situations that are important to us . . . even to use play objects to reenact a funeral that left us with deep feelings of loss. Though it sounds odd, and I doubt that many of us would feel comfortable doing so, we might possibly find it helpful.

As I think about that, I realize that's just what I felt I was doing during some of the hours I spent working with children at play. Their play would evoke past times in my own life, or make me think about times that were to come. I know that I grew a little more through those hours of play.

What gifts children so often bring us!

CHAPTER 4

ACTIVITIES: ME, YOU, & US

There's a growth task we all have to work through when we are very little, and that's the task of understanding that we are separate and distinct individuals . . . separate and distinct from everyone and everything else. At the very beginning of our lives, we felt a *oneness* with the people and things around us. "Me" was everything "me" encountered through sight, sound, smell, taste, and touch.

That journey from the feeling of oneness to the awareness of our separateness is a gradual journey. In fact, it's really never over. No matter how old we are, we still go on trying to understand our relationships with the people we love as well as with the world we live in. As we've suggested, though, it's the first three or four years of our lives that bring us the new awareness of our separateness and individuality. Those are the years during which we learn that we can say yes or no, that we can make choices about lots of things, that we can take something apart or put something together, that we can please or anger the people we love and who love us, and that we can find any number of ways to express the feelings that are ours and ours alone.

ACTIVITIES: ME, YOU, & US   41

In these early years, children may often need our support in their play, our encouragement to play out what they feel, and our quiet acknowledgment that their play is important enough to merit our time and interest. By letting our children know that we believe their play has value, we're letting them know that we believe *they* have value, too.

Display Ideas

It can be helpful to have a place to keep what children make. Children's pictures often find their way onto refrigerator doors or walls, but many times there just doesn't seem to be enough room to keep very many on display. Here are some suggestions that may help.

SCRAPBOOK   We specially liked one scrapbook we saw at the Galliucci's because it was big. In fact, it was huge. The pages were made of different colored construction paper. There were about thirty of them, and they measured about 14" from top to bottom, and about 24" from side to side. The book wasn't meant to be carried around all the time; instead, when Victor Jr. was little, it sat open on a homemade cardboard stand in one corner of his bedroom.

The stand has since disappeared, but the scrapbook still exists. It contains photos and drawings; letters, postcards and little made-up stories; different kinds of leaves; rubbings of dozens of things from a coin to a cantaloupe; art projects of many different kinds; and many other things besides.

The scrapbook has stiff cardboard covers, and they're cut from one fairly large box so that they are a little longer and wider than the pages that fit in between. As Victor Sr. recalled, he cut the covers so that they each came from one side of the box *plus* about two inches around the corner. In this way, each side had a hinged flap, and it was in these flaps that he and his son punched the holes for binding the book together. They punched three of them—one about three inches in from the top, another three inches in from the bottom, and the third right in between those two.

Next, they lined up the two covers with one piece of con-

struction paper carefully placed between them . . . and Victor Jr. held them tightly together as his father marked through the circles in the top cover. He helped young Victor punch out the marks, and then they used that first page to line up the rest of the pages—about three at a time. (They also saved the confetti-like pieces to use for another project later on.)

They bound their book together differently than we had seen before. They took a long piece of ¼″-wide ribbon and, having taped each end to make it easy to thread, they looped it around the bottom of the book, passed both ends through the first hole (in opposite directions), then back through the second, and back again through the top hole . . . and then they tied the ends of the ribbon in a bow across the very top of the book.

Once the book was bound, Victor asked his son if he wanted to decorate the cover. All he wanted to do was to print his name on the front. (As Victor Sr. mentioned, though, it would have probably been a good idea to ask about decorating the covers *before* binding the whole thing together.)

SCRAPBOOK STAND   Though Victor couldn't remember how he and his son had made the stand for the scrapbook, he did give us this suggestion, which he thought was fairly close to the original:

"Find a cardboard box that is just a little smaller in its dimensions than the scrapbook *when it's open*—a little less long and a little narrower. Draw a wide V on the long back of the box, one that starts at the top corners and meets in the middle about 3″ below the top edge. It's probably a good idea to flatten the bottom of the V just a bit, making it something like 1½″ across. That way, the spine of the scrapbook will rest in it a bit more comfortably.

"Then you want to work on the front long side of the box. I know we wanted the scrapbook to tilt a little toward the person looking at it, so I think we started by cutting 2″ down the two front corners . . . and then drawing exactly the same kind of V on the front that we had at the back. This time, though, the V started at the bottoms of the 2″ cuts. We flattened the point of that V, too. What we had at the end was two parallel Vs—one on the front and one on the back—with the front one being about 2″ lower than the back one. That difference was enough to tilt the open book . . . but not enough to make it slide off the stand onto the floor. As I recall, it worked fine, but maybe you'll think up some refinements of your own. If you do, be sure to let me know so that I can use them when it's time to make another scrapbook for a grandchild!"

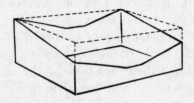

SHELVES Have you a wall somewhere to build four or five shelves? The easiest way, perhaps, is just to put plain pine or particle-board planks on cement blocks ... or bricks ... or milk crates. It can help to glue or nail a thin piece of molding the length of the planks—between the bricks or whatever—about two-thirds of the way toward the back. That piece of molding will let you lean some objects up against the wall without having them slip off the shelf, and you'll have room in front of them to put other things as well.

"Self" Projects

Here are some projects you could do with your child—projects that have something to do with a sense of *self*.

DRAWAROUND A drawaround is simply an outline of a child's body drawn on a large piece of paper. It's best to lay the paper out on the floor and have the child lie down on it—usually on his or her back, although you can invent other positions if you find them more interesting. You'll probably want to use a bold felt-tip marker of some kind, and once you've done the outline, you and your child can add any details you feel like, such as features on the face, fingernails, clothes and hair.

If you have trouble finding a piece of paper that's long and wide enough, you can make do with grocery bags that have been cut open, laid flat, and taped together. Even sheets of newspaper will work. Heavy brown paper, though, will most likely be the sturdiest and most practical.

If you keep your first drawaround, you can do another in a few months, and your child will be able to see how much he or she has grown. Rena Galliucci started making drawarounds with Rita when she was three. Rena cut out the first one and mounted it on the refrigerator door. She did the same with the second one, placing it behind the first so that the edges that showed made clear how much Rita had grown in the meantime. She kept on with these drawarounds until Rita literally "grew off the door" and the whole stack of drawarounds had to be moved to a wall in the basement.

By the time Becky was three, Rena had a new idea. She did the first drawaround in bright permanent color right on one of her daughter's bed sheets. Every few months, she'd do another in a different color on the same sheet, and of course it would be a little bigger than the last one. We weren't surprised to hear that the drawaround sheet became Becky's favorite!

HAND & FOOT CASTS   Bakers' clay, imprinted with a hand or foot, will dry overnight and can be painted and kept on a shelf. As with the drawaround, making these casts every few months, or every birthday, will clearly reveal a child's physical growth.

MEASURING POST   You can mark your child's height on a wall or door jamb—anywhere you don't mind making marks. Children often like to have their friends' heights marked in the same place—or the heights of other family members. It's useful to date and initial each mark so you can tell who it belongs to and when the mark was made. There are other important marks you might make, too—ones that signify your child's learning to share or to wait for a turn, learning to talk about feelings, learning to recognize letters and numbers, losing a tooth, having a birthday . . . all these are signs of growth as well.

FOOT & HAND PRINTS   You'll need lots of newspaper and a dishpan of soapy water right nearby for this colorful but messy project.

If you lay out a long piece of shelf paper (the white, shiny kind) on top of the newspaper that is covering the floor, you'll have a palette on which you can smear gobs of several colors of finger paint. Right alongside this palette, you can lay out another piece of shelf paper or paper of any color or texture you choose. Barefoot, your child can step into the paint and then off onto the other paper, making colored footprints any which way. You can add hand prints to the footprints, and fingerprints, too.

You may find that making one of these "murals" isn't enough—that by doing one, your child suddenly gets new ideas about how to do a second one differently. You may also find that when the prints are dry, your child wants to add new details in crayon or paint.

Do some of the footprints look like faces? Do the fingerprints look like anything else?

SELF-PORTRAITS   Children's own drawings of themselves can be interesting to collect as the months and years go by. (That's true of the pictures they make of you, too!) Whenever your child seems to be in a drawing mood, you could suggest a self-portrait and see what comes out. By dating them, you'll be able to see an unfolding sequence of a child's understanding of body parts and how they go together. The scrapbook might be a good place to keep these drawings.

COLLAGES Any time you have some old magazines around, you can hunt through them for things to cut out and paste on a piece of cardboard to make a collage. What you hunt for, of course, is up to you. It might be things your child likes best to eat . . . or things your child finds scary . . . or anything of a favorite color . . . or pictures of other children . . . or different expressions on people's faces.

TREASURE BOX Children often have special things that they've found or made or been given—anything from pebbles and shells to coins and toy cars. A child may find it reassuring to know that there is a place for these kinds of treasures, a place where they are safe and into which other people aren't supposed to go. Such a private box can help a child come to understand the concept of privacy in general—that it's something we all need for ourselves and something to respect in others.

A large match box (the kitchen size) may do for small objects, and children often like the way matchbox drawers slide in and out. Cookie tins with tight-fitting lids can work, as can any sturdy wooden or cardboard box. If you can find a box that has a latch or catch of some kind, so much the better. If you can't find one, perhaps you have an old belt with a buckle that your child can cinch around the box to give it an air of security. If the box is small enough, a thick rubber band may do the job.

Your child may have some strong feelings about how this special box is to be decorated—whether it has his or her name on it as well as any other messages such as, possibly, "private," or even "keep out." However the box takes shape, or whether it's just a particular drawer or particular space in a closet, what's most important is your acknowledgment that not everything in the child's world has to be shared with everybody else, and that it's all right to have a private treasure box.

SPECIAL FRIEND This Special Friend is nothing more than a pillowcase stuffed with anything soft—old rags, foam rubber, whatever. There are lots of ways, though, that you can give this friend an appealing personality (although its greatest appeal for your child may simply be your participation in its making). For

instance, whether you start with a patterned pillowcase or a plain one, you can sew bits of fabric onto it to give it a patchwork look—if that's what you decide you want.

You can tie the pillowcase shut at the top with some colorful yarn . . . and tie another piece around the middle to make a waist . . . and other pieces around each of the bottom corners to make "feet." How about buttons for eyes and a nose? (Just make sure they're *securely* fastened on.) And perhaps triangles or crescents of material for eyebrows and a mouth.

Do you want this friend to look happy or neutral or sad or angry? How would your child feel about having two different expressions on this friend—one on each side of the pillowcase?

You can make another shape by sewing the pillowcase closed at the top and tying yarn around the *top* corners to make "ears." You can still make feet if you want, but ears may be enough.

DYED PILLOWCASE If you are going to make a Special Friend out of a plain white pillowcase, you might want to think about dyeing it different colors. One way is to take a pole—a broom handle, for instance—drape the middle of the pillowcase over one end and pull it down around the pole, twisting it tight as you go. It will look sort of like a furled umbrella when you're done, and you'll need to hold the material in place with a piece of string or rubber band. In fact, you'll get the most interesting designs if you secure the cloth to the pole tightly in two or three different places.

Choose whatever colors of fabric dye you like, and then dab the furled pillowcase here and there with the dye solution. A couple of old paintbrushes might make good applicators. You'll want to be sure to wear some kind of smock and cover the surface you're working on with newspaper or plastic. Dye is permanent and can make a permanent mess!

If you're well protected, you can splash the dye around a little, and it's often the drops and splashes that make the best designs. When you think you're done, you can unfurl the pillowcase and see what you've made . . . and hang it up to dry.

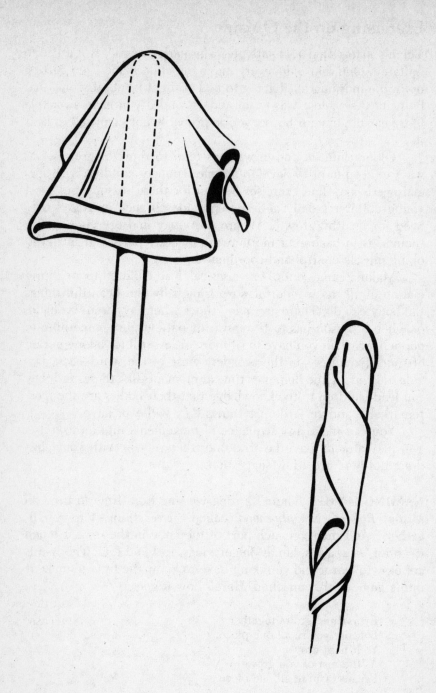

Exercising on the Outside

There's a story that a fine athlete in his early twenties was asked to imitate a four-year-old—every move the child made from getting up in the morning until going to bed at night. Well, it seems that by noon the athlete was exhausted ... and if you have an active four-year-old in your house, you're probably not surprised to hear it.

Older children and grown-ups tend to think of exercises as ways to keep fit or to develop muscle. Younger children with special needs may find exercises helpful for these reasons, but most young children's daily activities provide all the "exercise" they need for healthy growth. Where they may find exercises useful, though, is in becoming more aware of body parts and in developing muscle control and coordination.

Making games out of exercises can lead children to an appreciation of all the wonderful, surprising, silly and beautiful things the body can do. There are many times when toys aren't at hand, or when a person has to try and wait patiently for something to happen, or when you have to sit more or less still for a long period of time. Exercises—in the broadest sense of the word—can provide enjoyment and help pass time at moments like these, and they can lead children to the knowledge that their bodies are the most remarkable and versatile playthings they will ever have.

You can make any sequence of movements into an exercise. You may already have favorite ones that you do with your children, but here are a few suggestions.

NAMING GAME   There's a song we sing from time to time on *Mister Rogers' Neighborhood* called "Everything Grows Together." As I mention each part of the body in the song, I touch it—nose, ears, arms, hands, fingers, legs, feet and toes. The words are easy to learn, and you don't have to know the tune to make it into a game with your child. Here's how it goes:

> Everything grows together
> Because you're all one piece.
> Your nose grows
> As the rest of you grows
> Because you're all one piece.

Everything grows together
Because you're all one piece.
Your ears grow
As your nose grows
As the rest of you grows
Because you're all one piece.

Go on adding a new body part each verse—first arms, then hands, then fingers, and finally, legs. The final verse will go like this:

Everything grows together
Because you're all one piece.
Your toes grow
As your legs grow
As your fingers grow
As your hands grow
As your arms grow
As your ears grow
As your nose grows
As the rest of you grows
Because you're all one piece.

(If you feel like adding other body parts, you can certainly do that, too.)

MOVING PARTS   From head to toe, there are a lot of body parts! Discovering them and finding out how some move differently than others, and that we can control some better than others, is an activity that can last just about as long as you want it to.

We think it's more fun to start with the toes than with the head because that way the game ends up in making funny faces . . . and that usually ends up in laughter . . . which is a good way for any game to end.

"Can you wiggle your toes? Up and down? Side to side?

"Can you curl them up? Stretch them out? All together? One at a time?

"Can you move a big toe without moving the other toes on the same foot?

"Is there any other toe you can move like that?

"Can you move one big toe without moving the other big toe? Can you move both big toes the same way at the same time?

"Can you move each big toe in a different direction at the same time?"

As you move up the body, you'll probably get into talk about "left" and "right." Here's one friend's memory of that discovery:

I must have been about five years old, and my mother was helping me take a bath. For some reason we were talking about east and west—I think it was to do with where the sun came up and went down—and I was pointing east when she said, "Here, let me wash your right hand."

"My east hand," I said.

"Well," my mother said, "it's your east hand if you're sitting that way around, but if you turn the other way it will be your *west* hand."

"But will it still be my right hand?" I asked.

"It will always be your right hand," she said. "That never changes."

"But east and west never change, either," I said.

"No," she said, "they don't. But right and left are part of you, and they move around with you when you move. East and west are part of the world, and they stay where they are."

It didn't come clear to me all at once. I remember playing with that idea for quite some time, practicing pointing in different directions and checking to make sure that my right hand was still *right*. I remember, too, figuring out that right and left for me weren't always in the same directions that they were for other people.

In playing with that puzzle I arrived at a whole new awareness of my independence and separateness—both from the world of things and from the world of people.

FINGER GAMES   You may have finger games that you remember from your childhood. Here are a few that we remember:

• Starting with your fingers intertwined—but with the fingers *inside*, pointing down and hidden between the palms—you say:
"Here is the church . . ."
Then, raising your two index fingers into a point, you go on:
". . . and here is the steeple."

Next you rotate your hands away from you, letting your index fingers intertwine again, revealing all your fingers. As you do so, you say:

"Open the doors and see all the people!"

(You can wiggle your fingers around a bit if you want to so that the "people" will look lively.)

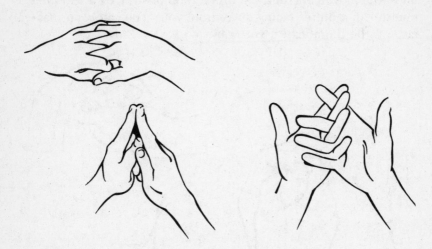

This next part may be less familiar to you.

You cross your wrists one over the other, palms down, and link first your little fingers, then third, second and index. As you're doing the linking, you say: "Here is the minister going up stairs . . ."

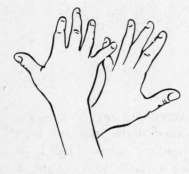

Now here's the tricky part. Rotate the bottom wrist and hand so that the two wrists separate. Hang on tight and keep going slowly, and you'll find that your elbows will swing out from your body and allow your hands to go down away from you, around and up again next to your chest. With a little experimentation, you'll find that one thumb tends naturally to encircle the other as you finish the movement, and the inside thumb will look a little like a minister in a pulpit facing away from you. (You can even make a face on the thumbnail if you want to.)

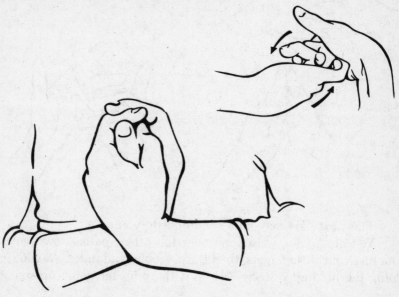

As you're doing this last movement, you say:
". . . and here is the minister saying his prayers!"

• You can make four-legged creatures with long necks—dinosaurs, maybe. They can do exercises, too. Can they raise one leg at a time? Both front legs at once? One front and one hind leg? If you make one with each hand, do they have anything to say to one another?

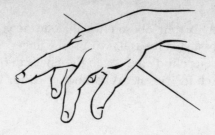

• You can make geese or swans. What can *they* do? Any ideas for a story about dinosaurs and swans? You could try making up a tag story with your child (*see p. 164*). You might find you both come up with something you'd like to write down and put in the scrapbook.

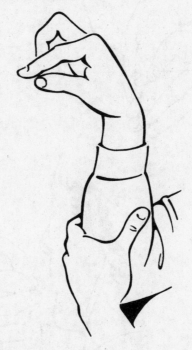

• Stretch your arms out in front of you with your thumbs pointing down. Now cross your arms so that the palms of your hands are against each other. Interweave your fingers and clasp them tightly. Bring your hands down and around so that they come up close to your chest and your elbows are together. If your child points to (but doesn't touch) one of your fingers, can you wiggle that one? Is it easier with some fingers than with others? Is it easier if your child *does* touch the finger in question? How about when your child tries it? Who finds it easier to move the correct finger?

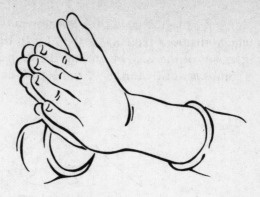

• You can make a "wiggle-waggle" by putting your hands together in the "prayer" shape, crossing the middle fingers (right farthest from you, left closest to you), slowly rotating your right hand toward you and your left away from you . . . Now you can wigglewaggle.

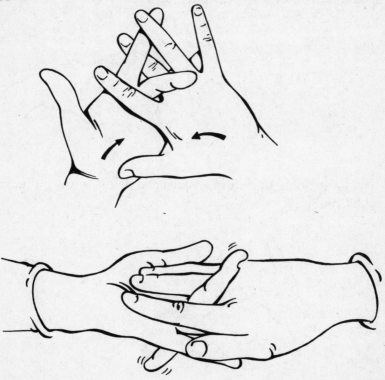

• To play "inchworm": Start by putting your thumbs together and your index fingers together, tip to tip, keeping your other fingers out of the way by curling them up in your palms. Hold your thumbs against your chest and start "inching" by

—bringing your left thumb up to the left index finger (both should now be at the tip of the right index finger);

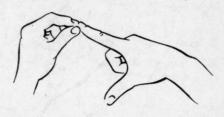

—extending the left index finger so that it is way out in front all by itself;

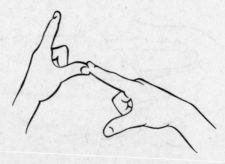

—bringing the right thumb up to the right index finger (both should now be at the tip of the left thumb);

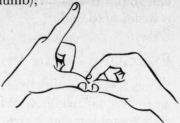

—extending the right index finger to meet the left index finger tip to tip;
—and starting the process again.

Only the hand that is doing the inching should move. The other should stay absolutely still—and that may not be easy at first. This way, as you inch, your hands will get farther and farther away from you until they're stretched out at arms' length. At that point, you can reverse the process and start inching back toward your chest where you started.

Some people like to start with their hands down low and pointing upward so that inching takes their hands up in front of their face and up over their head. Which do you prefer?

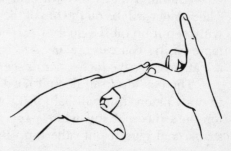

• Do you remember how much practice it took for you to be able to pat your head and rub your stomach at the same time? Or is it *still* hard to do?

Exercising on the Inside

So much of our ability to learn and do "outside" activities depends on an "inside" readiness. We've all known times when we couldn't seem to get something right no matter how hard we tried . . . and then, at a later moment, it came to us without much difficulty at all. It's hard to say what this readiness is, but it's something we can certainly feel—just as we can see it happening again and again with children in their early years. One day a task is beyond their capabilities, and the next day they've mastered it.

Inside readiness has a lot to do with developing self-control. For children, particularly, learning self-control means learning such things as taking turns, sharing, accepting limits, waiting, working cooperatively, trying again and again, and putting things away where they belong. Almost all forms of play give a child a chance to practice one or more of these abilities, but there's one toy, a "spinner," that lends itself to so many kinds of games that it's somewhat like a passkey. A spinner also requires that people take turns, and it naturally tends to impose limits that can take a good deal of self-control to observe.

There is another thing about spinners: they get a good deal of wear and tear, so it's worth a little time and effort to make a sturdy one. Here's a suggestion for making one—an activity all by itself.

SPINNER You can start with the top of a heavy cardboard box—the kind that fits down over the box's bottom on all sides. The spinner will be on the top of the box, and the flaps on the sides will keep it up off the floor or carpet so that the spinner will spin more easily. You can use any size box top you like, but ones that are at least twelve inches across seem easiest to handle.

The box top itself doesn't need to be square. When it comes to drawing on it, it will help if it's white. You can always set the top on a piece of stiff white paper, draw around it, cut out the shape, and glue it onto the top. (Be sure to use plenty of glue,

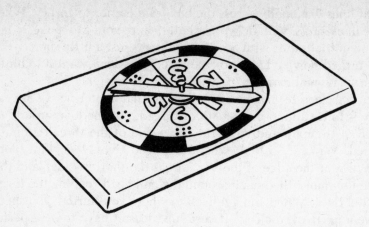

especially around the edges, and look to see if the instructions on the glue you're using say to cover both surfaces or just one.)

When the paper covering is in place, you might want to turn the spinner upside down on a flat surface and put something heavy and flat inside—books perhaps—to keep the two surfaces pressed tightly together while the glue is drying.

So far, you've probably had some chance for "inside" exercises on cooperation! Could your child help hold the box top steady while you drew around it? Or hold the paper steady while you cut out the shape? Or help spread on the glue?

Waiting for glue to dry interrupts any activity such as this one . . . but there's nothing to do but wait. Learning to wait and to fill in the time is another good exercise, and it's one that's often not easy for many of us.

This might be a good time to talk about having to stop and wait when you're in the middle of doing something that you want to go on doing. It can be reassuring to children to hear that you know how hard that can be. You could talk about other times when people have to wait as well: when you have to wait for tomorrow to do something you want to do; or wait for someone who's been away to come home again; or even wait when you're mad and feel like hitting someone or throwing something.

One of the best parts of playing together can be the chances you find for talking!

When the glue is dry enough so that you can continue, you'll need to find the center of the box top. You can do this by drawing light lines diagonally across the box from corner to corner. Where the lines cross will be your center, and you can poke a hole through that point with a nail—one that's just a little shorter than the turned-down edges of the box top. (You don't want it to hit the floor.) The nail can stay right there in the center.

You need to make a circle around that center now. One easy way is to tie a loop in a length of thread, put the loop around the head of the nail, and wrap the other end of the thread around a pencil. Wrap it so that, with the thread tight, the point of the pencil is at the edge of the box top (at the shortest side), and then carefully move the pencil around the nail head keeping the thread pulled tight. When you get back to where you started, you should have a fairly even circle. It certainly doesn't have to be a perfect one.

This circle needs to be divided into six roughly equal pie-shaped wedges. You can do it by eye if you like, but a wristwatch can help you so long as it's got numbers around the face instead of a digital readout. All you have to do is put the watch in the center of the circle, and, with a straightedge of any kind, mark where the line through 12 and 6 hits the circle's edge; and then the line through the 2 and the 8; and then the line through the 4 and the 10. Once you've drawn lines connecting the marks on the circle's edge to the center of the circle, you should have what you need.

There are lots of different things you can do with these wedges in the way of making them useful for games you have or might want to make up. One spinner we've seen was full of possibilities, and we'll describe it here even though you may prefer to make it simpler or to do it differently altogether.

To begin with, it had a circle within the big circle—one that left a border around the edge about an inch wide. Each section of the border (the widest part of the pie-shaped wedges) was divided in half, and one half was red and the other was green. That's the way it was all around the edge: alternating patches of red and green.

The other part of each wedge was painted a different color of the rainbow. One was red, and then, in sequence, they went orange, yellow, green, blue and purple. And on each color was a large number from 1 to 6 and a corresponding number of dots. (The dots were just to help young children associate the two ways of expressing numbers.) On the spinner we saw, the numbers had been cut out of a calendar, so they looked very exact and neat, but you could just as well paint them on (or use colored marking pens) once the color underneath is dry.

The spinning arm was a white arrow cut from cardboard. It had a hole in its middle just big enough for the nail to pass through easily. There were two washers stacked between the arm and the box top's surface, and another between the arm and the head of the nail. A little soap rubbed on the washers that touched the spinning arm worked as a good lubricant. And the arrow's point reached right out to the red and green border at the edge of the circle.

SPINNER GAMES   A simple game you could play with a spinner like that would be a stop-and-go game with a toy car. You could put some blocks here and there around the floor, start at any one you like, and move to another each time the spinner points to green. If it points to red, then the other person takes a turn and moves from block to block, spinning each time, until red comes up . . . and so forth.

You could play the same sort of game using a checkerboard if you have one handy. If you place a checker or button or marker or toy car or whatever on any square on the edge of the board, you can see how many turns it takes you to get clear across to the opposite edge—one square at a time and only moving when your spin comes up green.

You could use the numbers on the spinner, too, of course. If your spin comes up "4" and "green," you might get to move four squares ahead. But if it comes up "4" and "red," then you might decide that you either couldn't move . . . or even that you had to go *backwards* four squares (or back to the edge of the board, whichever comes first).

You and your playing partner could start on *adjacent* sides of the board. That way, as you both make your way across, there's a chance you might bump into each other. You could make a rule that if you did, you both had to go back to where you started and begin all over again.

As for the colors . . . well, they'd be useful for sorting games, for instance. If you have a pile of different colored objects—beads, say—you could take turns spinning and picking up an object of the same color that you land on. Or the same number of them that corresponds with the number on the colored wedge. Or you might pick up just one, but it might be worth that number of points.

You could take the spinner outdoors and make a game out of trying to get to a certain tree. Red and green and the numbers would tell you how many paces you could move ahead—or not move at all, or move backwards.

If you're playing outdoors, can you find anything around that's the same color as the color that comes up when it's your turn on the spinner? Indoors, you could look for those colors in old magazines or in objects around the house.

In the Galliucci household, a simple spinner with numbers and red and green wedges became the source of a bedtime game. Stefano and Victor Jr. were six and four, and neither one wanted to go to bed when it was time. They could think up all sorts of ways to stall and wheedle. One evening their father suggested using the spinner to see how fast they had to go upstairs: green and a number meant they had to go *up* that many steps, and red and a number allowed them to come back *down* that many.

"I don't remember it ever taking more than about ten minutes for them to wind up upstairs," Victor told us, "but the game made a lot of difference in how they felt about getting there. Rena and I would act super disappointed whenever a red came up. The kids, of course, were delighted—particularly if a red saved them right at the last step to the top. I guess they knew that eventually they'd 'lose' and have to go to bed, but so long as there was a lot of seesawing back and forth, they kind of felt they'd won all the same. The game allowed them to stall for a while, and we were able to turn that difficult moment for bedtime into something we all enjoyed."

Some Other Ideas

MAKING A MAP It takes a while for children to begin understanding where different places are in relationship to one another. For very young children, people are either here . . . or *not* here. When they go away, they're simply *gone*. Little by little, though, they come to realize that people go away to different places and that they come back again. It's another step for them to realize that all these places that people go are connected by streets and highways, by train tracks, and airways. Making a map of places your child knows about can be one way to help foster the reassuring knowledge that all people and places are in some way connected.

The place you live is a good starting point on your map. You may want to use an extra-large piece of paper, too—particularly if you decide to put lots of places on it or add to it from time to time.

How could you identify your home? You could write "our house," draw a picture of it, use a snapshot of it or of your family, cut out a picture of a similar house, or some other way you think of.

What's nearby? Local stores you go to, a school, a post office, friends' houses you walk to, a playground or park . . .

What's farther away? The places Mom and Dad go to work, a doctor's office, friends' houses you visit by car or a shopping mall . . .

What's really far away? Where grandparents live, where friends have moved to, places you've been on vacation . . .

Can you find ways to mark all these places? How are they connected, and how would you get there and back?

If you have a place where you can keep your map spread out, you may find your child will enjoy playing about all this coming and going—especially about the times and ways that the important people in his or her life come home again!

PAPER WINDOWS   Any game that suggests peek-a-boo is often a popular one with young children, and pleasant surprises remain a delight for most of us all our lives. Here's an activity that can combine both.

You can start by drawing one big window on a piece of paper. All it needs to be is a large square or rectangle. If you cut it part-way down the middle and part-way across the top and bottom, you'll have two flaps that open from the center.

Now, you can tape or glue a second piece of paper behind the first—any color you like, but at least large enough to fit over the window that you've already made. Once the second sheet is in

place, you can draw on it or perhaps make a collage. When you're done, you can play shutting the window . . . opening the window . . . now you see it . . . now you don't.

You could try a second version—this time drawing several windows on the first sheet. If some are small, you don't have to cut them down the center; it will be enough to cut around three sides so that there's just one single flap to open and shut. When you've made your drawings and shut the windows, can your child remember what drawing is behind which window?

With older children, you might want to go a step further, using a wall calendar that has a good-size square for each day of the month. Not all of the squares in a month have to become windows; you may want to do just ones that are special events, such as birthdays, arrivals, departures, or something to look forward to. In addition to using drawings as "window dressings," you might want to consider cutouts from magazines or even parts of family snapshots.

Any family members who want to can take turns making a window calendar such as this. Each month could be full of surprises for the rest of the family.

DOLL HOUSE   Any large open box that's fairly deep can be a doll house. You'll probably want to cut a few windows and a door in the sides, because part of the fun of toy houses is looking into them from the point of view of someone small enough to live there. Do you think your house needs a paint job?

With two similar boxes, you can have a two-story house—so long as the sizes and shapes allow one box to sit on top of the other. If you're going to use them this way, the openings on the ground floor will need to be big enough to get furniture in and out. And if you want a peaked roof, two adjoining sides of a third box should do the trick.

Two boxes can also make two separate houses, and you could use them for pretending about moving from one place to another. (That could be an important kind of play if your family is *really* planning a move.) You don't need a fancy moving truck. One we saw was a shoebox attached to a roller skate. It could have been just the shoebox *or* the roller skate. It could have been a shoe, too. How about an egg carton (*see page 181*)?

DOLL-HOUSE FURNITURE   The tops and bottoms of very small cardboard boxes can be fitted together, even without glue, to make a variety of furniture shapes. Generally, if you place the bottom of the box upside down for the seat, you'll find that the top will fit, vertically, along one of the sides to form the back. If you want the chair or sofa or lounge chair to be sturdier, you may choose to glue the parts together . . . and to paint them or cover them with fabric.

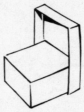

Little boxes make good beds, too. You can fill them with cotton wrapped in a scrap of material and use another scrap as a blanket. Very small scraps, stuffed with cotton and sewn shut with a few stitches, can become pillows. Before you throw away some worn-out gloves next time, you might save the finger parts, stuff them with cotton, sew the ends shut, and use them as bolsters.

Four equal lengths of drinking straws—one glued inside each corner of a box bottom—turns a simple bed into a four poster. The top of the box should be able to fit over the tops of the straws and act as a canopy.

Thread spools are good end tables. With a piece of flat cardboard stuck on top, they can be dining-room tables as well.

Spools can be useful in other ways. You can stick a pole in their center (a stiff cotton swab, perhaps, or the tapered end of a pencil stub) and make a lamp by gluing a deep-sided, twist-off bottle cap to the end of the pole. (These kinds of bottle caps are often found on 32-ounce pop bottles.) You could use a small paper or foil baking cup instead, but you might find yourself ending up with something that looks more like a patio umbrella than a lamp. There's nothing the matter with that, though; it can be whatever you say it is.

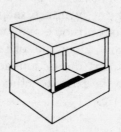

CHAPTER 5

THOUGHTS:
PLAY
&
INDEPENDENCE

One of the mysterious things about growing is how we grow from dependence to independence. Most everyone comes to an awareness of complete physical independence, but emotional independence is an altogether different matter. Some people seem to achieve so little emotional independence that their need for dependence gets in the way of their becoming all that they could be. Others may grow to feel so emotionally isolated that they can't seem to form deep relationships that mean depending on someone else at all. Most of us seem to end up somewhere in between, but just where within that wide range we land is part of what makes each of us different from one another.

The puzzle of how dependent and independent they are—and how dependent and independent they want to be—is one of the biggest puzzles that children work on in their earliest years. It's not always obvious to us what they're doing, but puzzling it out is a large part of their play. Patting their images in a mirror is part of it. So is their attachment to a special blanket or teddy bear. Thumb sucking, too, and those sudden returns to you for a hug after crawling or toddling off a ways to explore. Throwing things out of the playpen again and again, or down from a high chair, is part of it, as are the repeated "no's" that two-year-olds come up with. Playing the part of grown-ups by caring for dolls, or walking around in a grown-up's shoes are signs of it, as are all the times that children use their play to practice being in control of a make-believe situation. Times that seem like defiance may be ways to say, "Look how independent I can be!" So often these are matched by times of acting younger again—of clinging, whining or even wetting—as if to reassure themselves that it's still all right to be as dependent as they sometimes still feel.

Just after one of our visits to the Galliuccis many years ago, Tony Warninski happened to come over to help his brother-in-law, Victor, with an automobile repair job. In the course of their conversation, Victor asked two-and-a-half-year-old Becky, "Did you tell Uncle Tony that Mister Rogers came to visit you?" Becky turned to her uncle and said, "Mister Rogers came to visit you." Then she added, "To visit *me*." When Victor told us that, I remember thinking it sounded to me like Becky had found another little piece of the independence puzzle.

Of course it's one thing to know that you're independent, and it's quite another to know how you feel about being the independent person you are. Are you pleased with yourself? Do you feel valuable and valued? Whether we do or not probably depends more than on anything else on whether or not we feel loved by the people we have come to love. For us, their faces are like mirrors. If, when they look at us, we see joy and delight in their eyes and their smiles, we're likely to feel pleasure in being who we are. That's one way healthy self-image grows. And when those "mirrors" around us reflect anger, disgust or displeasure, we may feel very badly about who we are. That's why it's always so important when we get mad at our children to let them know it's not *they* who are bad but only whatever it is that they've done. It's truly an important difference to try to make clear as a child's self-image is developing, and it's one we need to emphasize over and over again as our children are growing. Can you still feel some uncertainty about that difference in your life when you've done something "bad" (as we all do)? I know I can!

Wanting to be loved by those we love . . . and fearing that we may lose that love . . . these are such big motivations in doing the things we do and becoming the people we are! One of the places you can often see these forces at work in children's play is in competition. Why can winning and losing at a game arouse such deep, deep feelings?

In early childhood—and even well beyond—I believe the issue is love, the love of those around us which keeps us secure in our feelings of self-worth. Later on, we might want to call it an issue of esteem—the esteem of the fans in the stadium, for instance, that can keep us secure in our feelings of self-esteem.

It seems to me that it's those people who have grown to feel secure about their value to the people they care about who can tolerate the disappointment of losing a game without feeling diminished themselves . . . or who can cope with the elation of winning a game without becoming "swell-headed" . . . or who can accept an umpire's impartial decision without feeling put down . . . or who can resist the temptations we're all offered to cheat our ways to a victory. But for young children at play, I believe it's love, and the fear of losing that love by losing a game, that's the real issue.

Early competitive play gives children chance after chance to see how they feel about winning and losing. And it gives fortunate children chance after chance to find out that by losing a game they aren't risking losing love. Children who find that out when they are young are the ones, I believe, who are most likely to grow into adults who can find satisfaction and pleasure in doing the best they can in any competition—win, lose or draw.

CHAPTER 6

ACTIVITIES: PRETENDING & PUPPETS

Carrie, Taylor and Alex are seven, five and three. Nan and David Newell are their mother and father. Nan has helped us in many ways with *Mister Rogers' Neighborhood* and the work of Family Communications, and David is our Director of Public Relations, as well as the character, Mr. McFeely—"Speedy Delivery"—in the Neighborhood.

The three Newell children like to pretend together, Nan tells us. When they do, they have other names that they've made up for themselves: Kathy, Bill, and Mike. These three pretend children play out many different things together, but one part of the play is usually the same: they haven't any parents because both parents have died.

A grown-up friend of ours remembers that when he was little he used to pretend that he was Mandrake the Magician—a popular newspaper comic strip at that time. "I could spend hours in a land of my own, inventing problems and solving them through the power of a magic ring. It seems like it went on for years, my Mandrake play. I remember that when I began losing my baby teeth I would put each one under my pillow, and in the morning I'd find a new magic ring, and I'd pretend it could do all sorts of new magical things."

Eric and Teri Hayes had an elaborate toy village where they used to do a lot of pretending. A constant character in their play was called "The Master Planner." This character was never seen, but was without question the authority when it came to how the village should be built or what should happen there. The two children would often disagree about the direction their play should take, and their squabbles could be bitter and intense. But whenever one or the other brought in The Master Planner, they were able to agree.

"No, we can't do that because The Master Planner doesn't like it," one of the children might protest in response to the other's suggestion. Or, "We have to pretend this is a hotel because The Master Planner wants us to," one or the other might say. At that time they just didn't question The Master Planner.

Looking back, the children's parents recalled that for a long time it was only Eric, the elder of the two, who seemed to know what The Master Planner wanted or didn't want. Little by little, though, Teri came to realize that two could play that game ... and then still later, the two children began squabbling over just what The Master Planner *did* want and whose turn it was to be The Master Planner, anyway.

And imaginary friends! We've known of so many children with imaginary animal or human friends—naughty ones and good ones, angry ones and loving ones, scary ones or reassuring ones. They can play an endless number of roles and fill dozens of different needs, acting as the companion and participant in countless pretend adventures. And then, suddenly, they're likely to vanish as unexpectedly as they turned up. Often, in later years, it's only the parents who remember that these imaginary friends were once part of the family at all.

Although pretending can take such a lot of different forms, most of it seems a way of trying things out—whether it be trying out what it would be like to be a princess or a pilot, to be children without parents, to be able to solve problems magically, to be in control of who does what and when, or to have a faithful friend who will always do what you say or take the blame for what goes wrong. A lot of times children use their pretending to try out

things that will never happen or can't come true, but at other times they use their make-believe to find out how they feel about something they know *is* going to happen—like moving to a new home and leaving old friends behind. Or they may use their make-believe to help them become more comfortable with the feelings they have about something that already did happen—a trip to the emergency room, say, for a broken leg or stitches.

Perhaps feelings are what pretending is mostly about. "How would it feel if . . . ?" is one large source of make-believe, but real, actual and present feelings are another: "How does it really feel to feel the way I do?"

Most children fall into pretending very naturally by the time they're a year or so old. They may pretend that a doll or a teddy bear is taking a bath or going to bed or being fed. These are big events in the life of a toddler who, through this kind of make-believe, may come to feel a little more secure that you really can't go down the drain in the tub, and that nighttime separations really will be followed by morning reunions.

In fact, pretending comes so naturally to children that most need some help from the grown-ups who care for them in keeping clear what is pretend and what is real. It's only when children have a firm sense of the difference that they can dare pretend about scary or sad things that they may need to try out. Have you ever seen a child get upset by his or her own make-believe when it got to seem a little too real? It can be like a bad dream when pretending gets out of control, and children often do need reminders from us that their make-believe is up to them: they can start and stop pretending whenever they want, and they can set their own limits on what they feel comfortable pretending about.

(Many parents have had the experience of helping their children make Halloween costumes, costumes their children asked for, only to find that the costumes turned out to be too scary for their children to wear: the creature or monster just seemed too real.)

One thing our children need to know for sure is that wishing can't make things happen—not good things and not bad things. There will be times when they do wish for something and it does happen, and it's easy for them to believe that their wishing had something to do with it. They need to know that when a good thing happens, it was a real person or real people somewhere who made it happen—not by wishing but by *doing.* And we need to help them understand, too, that life is full of accidents and illnesses that we can neither prevent nor cause by wishing *or* doing.

The importance of pretending stays with us all our lives. It's the old bond that unites actors and audiences alike wherever someone is telling a story and someone is listening. Most of us have "acts" we put on for the other people in our lives, the people we work with and the people we play with, and often we find ourselves "dressing the part" when we need to impress someone else or meet their expectations. And of course almost all of us continue to fantasize and daydream and imagine what it might be like to be someone else at another time in another place . . . or what we'd do if we won the lottery. In the course of our daily lives, we may pretend we are more secure than we are, or happier than we are, or that we don't care about something we *do* care about—or even some*one* we do care about.

We need to pretend, just as our children do, and for many of the same reasons—to try out, to get relief, to rehearse for the future or to become more comfortable with the past. As we do so, though, we have to keep a firm sense of where the pretending ends and real life begins. That's a line which, if we were fortunate, our earliest caregivers helped us establish when we were very, very young.

In *Mister Rogers' Neighborhood* we use puppets for a lot of our pretend. Here are some thoughts about their use that you might want to consider in your play at home.

PUPPET STAGE   Arenas for puppet play are likely to evolve from virtually nothing in the way of a stage to quite an elaborate affair that includes a curtain that opens, a backdrop and other theatrical trappings. The same is true of the puppets with which a child may feel comfortable. A wooden spoon with a face painted on it may be just fine for a while . . . and then later your child may become quite interested in puppets that fit over the hand. Marionettes that hang from strings take a lot more skill to manipulate, but if you have the chance to take your child to a marionette theater, you may find that he or she suddenly wants to start making simple ones at home.

The same kind of progression holds true with the stories that these characters act out. To begin with, they may be adventures of only a few sentences that deal with getting up, going to bed, eating or other daily routines such as going to the store. Sometimes, at the beginning, these stories may be hectic and rambling and may not seem to make much sense. You can be sure, though, that the stories *do* have some kind of logic from the child's point of view—even if the "logic" is simply an expression of the child's inner feelings that there is lots about the world that doesn't make much sense as yet.

It may be tempting for us as we play with our children to hasten the growth from simple to intricate in their puppet play . . . but we need to be wary about doing that. We can certainly suggest and encourage and demonstrate different ways to engage in puppet play, but what we need to do most of all is to show interest and support for whatever form seems comfortable for our children at the time. It is children's inner readiness that lets their play develop in length and complexity, and that readiness can't be hurried. To try to do so is to risk bringing this valuable kind of play to a halt altogether.

The first puppet play isn't likely to have a stage at all. It's likely to be just a puppet in or on a hand, or maybe even a teddy bear, or doll that one of you pretends can talk.

The first "stage" is likely to be your body as one day you put on a hand puppet and hold it in the crook of your arm. Here's the beginning of illusion. The puppet doesn't seem to be on your hand; it seems to have a life of its own. You may notice your child starting to relate to it differently than before—a little more confidentially, perhaps. Puppet play moves naturally from there to table tops. The puppeteers may still be in full sight, sitting next to one another on the same side of the table, but their elbows and arms can be below the level of the table so that the puppets seem to stand and move along the table's edge. This is a time when you may find props creeping into the play—an animal or a house or a car or a stick that might represent just about anything.

The play may evolve again as the table gets draped with a sheet or blanket, and the puppeteer sits behind it, entirely out of sight, holding only the puppets in view. You may find that hiding behind a sofa works well . . . or crouching down behind a sheet

tacked across a doorway. Before long, you're likely to find that you need an audience. Your child may be a willing audience as you manipulate two puppets, one on each hand, who talk not only to one another but to your child as well. But of course your child may enjoy being a puppeteer, too—alone or with you—and together you could make up stories for other family members and friends to watch. Soon, there's likely to come a time when your child (along with some friends, perhaps) makes up stories for *you* to watch from out front.

As you see your child's play taking on independence and confidence, you may want to suggest making a stage for puppet play. A tried-and-true method is to use a heavy cardboard appliance box such as a refrigerator might come in—one that is tall and sturdy.

You can cut out the top, one side and the bottom so that what you have left is three walls. When you cut the bottom, though, it's a good idea to leave tabs about 6" wide attached to the walls so that you can tack or tape the walls to the floor . . . or you can simply put bricks on the tabs if you're not in a place where tacks or tape are practical.

In the top third of the center cardboard wall you can cut an opening for the stage. It might come to within 3" of the edge on the top and sides of the wall.

Some people like to make a curtain that slides across the opening on a wire or thin dowel. All it takes is a piece of cloth with a hem in it and two fasteners such as small eye screws. Other people we know have covered the opening with a window shade mounted on the inside that could be pulled down between acts or at the end of the show. One advantage to the window shade is that you can paint something on it if you like.

You can, of course, make backdrops, too. Old sheets or other large pieces of material, if you have them, are easier to handle than large sheets of paper that are almost certain to tear, but either will do. The backdrops can be fancy or plain, scenes or shapes, whatever you feel like making them.

And you can decorate the front of the stage to make it look as theatrical as you want to . . . or just stick lots of scraps of paper all over to make it look festive.

Children are likely to be six or so before they can really make use of a stage as "official" as the one above. If you find that puppet play happens most easily when you're sitting close to each other, holding puppets in the crooks of your arms . . . then you've already found the best stage of all.

Making Puppets

There's no way we know to predict that a certain toy, doll, animal or puppet will suddenly become a child's favorite—or even be liked at all. Aunt Jane's expensive and beautiful birthday doll may end up in a corner all alone, ignored by her new owner and by all the raggedy characters who are already part of a child's ongoing fantasy play. But then, a week, month or even a year later, that new doll may be accepted into the charmed circle and become a truly cherished companion.

Being homemade is no guarantee of popularity, but whatever you and your child create together may take on particular significance because of its association with you. Most important, it seems, is whether or not a puppet takes on a character that expresses some of a child's inner needs at the time. That's one reason why it may be well to let your child decide what kind of character a new puppet is to become.

As you're making a puppet, you'll have plenty of time to talk about its growing personality, and that's the way we've found it best to encounter a puppet for the first time: to talk *about* it.

As your puppet nears completion, it's going to seem natural to start talking *to* it. You may find you or your child saying, "Now you hold still while your glue dries!" or asking the puppet how it feels about finishing touches: "How about a button for your nose, huh? How do you feel about that?" Once you find yourselves talking to the puppet, it's only a matter of time before one of you starts talking *for* the puppet and answering back. By the time that happens, you'll have brought into being a fairly well-developed new character who may already seem somewhat of an old friend.

Here are some different kinds of puppets you might find it fun to make in your own way.

SPOON PUPPETS   Long-handled wooden spoons are our favorites for these kinds of puppets just because of the way they feel, but large serving spoons work fine, too. (Depending on what kind of paint you use, wooden surfaces may also turn out to be easier to paint on.)

You can paint faces directly on the surface of the spoon—on either the bulging side or the scooped side. Or you can paint two faces, each with a different expression, one on one side and one on the other. If you like, you can glue some cotton balls or yarn around the rim to make hair. A double-faced spoon may mystify a toddler for a while. How do the expressions change so fast, from happy to sad, or from asleep to awake, or whatever? In fact, toddlers may scrutinize these spoon puppets very intently. When they're playing with them themselves, you'll probably have to

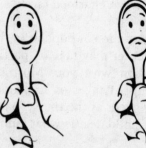

help them understand that these kinds of spoons are not meant for putting in their mouths. Because they're almost certain to try, be sure that whatever paint you use is clearly marked *nontoxic*.

Spoon puppets can become quite elaborate if you want them to. For instance, you can take a handkerchief or square of any old fabric and drape it over the spoon, stuffing cotton balls into the scoop and tying the fabric tight around the narrow neck of the handle with a piece of yarn or trash-bag twist. This way, you'll have a somewhat egg-shaped head for your puppet. You'll also have a ruffled collar, or, if the piece of fabric you use is big enough, even a skirt.

When it comes to making a face for this puppet, you may find it easier to mark off the area on the fabric where you want the face to be (once you've draped it over the spoon and cotton stuffing), then take the fabric off again and work with it flat on a table. This way you can even make the features out of buttons or scraps of other material. You might find it interesting, too, to make the head out of one piece of material and the skirt out of a second, contrasting piece. If you decide to try this, you'll want to cut a little hole in the center of the square that's to become the skirt so that it can fit over the handle of the spoon. (It's up to you whether this separate skirt fits under or over the ruffled collar below the puppet's face.)

The most elaborate spoon puppets we've seen were made by Martha Warninski for a Christmas bazaar at her son's preschool.

She made a dozen of them, and, incidentally, they sold out. Here's what she did:

She started with wooden spoons and made fabric heads stuffed with cotton. She generally used buttons for features, but she also found some of those toy "eyes" that have black centers that roll around on white backgrounds. She made contrasting skirts for the puppets, but because she wanted some to be male, she made one into a sorcerer with gold stars stuck on a black robe (he also had a pointed hat made out of a cone of black paper), and others she made from rough fabrics such as denim and burlap.

She then made the puppets into double-ended pairs by tying the handles of any two together with about a 6" overlap. (Below, you'll find an illustration of her way of attaching them together.) Most of them ended up being just two different faces—one on

each end—but she tried a couple with *two* different faces on each end (front and back) so that she had one single toy with four characters on it. She enjoyed making them that way, but she admitted that they were a little complicated to use except for parents and older children.

STICK PUPPETS   Representations of people or animals, stuck on the end of a stick, are another basic form of puppet. Although they are simple, they can be used a number of ways and become adaptable to the abilities of children at different ages. If the puppets are very light weight, you can even mount them on drinking straws.

For instance, you might want to make a paper-bird puppet. One way to do so is to fold a piece of paper in half and draw the outline of a bird on one side—leaving at least 3½″ of the bird's tummy running along the fold. When you've cut out the outline, you'll have two bird shapes that are joined along that tummy section. In the middle of that section, cut a hole that's just large enough to let a drinking straw pass through. The straw will be the handle for the puppet, and you'll probably want to have about 1″ of the straw glued in between the two birds. You can also glue the

birds' two heads and two tails together, but you may want to bend the wings outwards in opposite directions to make it look like the bird is in flight. How do you want to decorate the bird puppet? The same on both sides, or different?

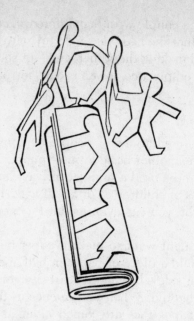

If you wanted to make a paper-person puppet, you could start by making a short chain of paper dolls. You may already know a way to do this, but here's one suggestion. Fold a piece of paper in half . . . and then in half again in the same direction . . . and once more. Three folds in all. One side will be open, and the other side will be a continuous fold. Starting somewhere along the fold, draw the outline of half a person. You might want to make one outline with pants, and one with a skirt.

If you want your paper dolls to be joined hand to hand, it's important to run the arm of your outline clear off the far edge of the paper. When you've cut out your outline and unfolded it, you should have four people in a chain—all, of course, nearly identical. If you now separate them into twos, each set of two can become a single two-sided puppet by folding the one figure on top of the other and gluing a drinking straw in between—just as we suggested for the paper-bird puppet. With crayons or paint, you can give your paper people any kind of features and clothes you like. And the figures wearing pants certainly don't *have* to be the boys.

Pictures on sticks can give you an endless variety of puppets. The pictures could be ones your child draws, or they could be cut-outs from magazines. They could even be family snapshots. Whatever you use, you may find it helpful to trace around it onto a piece of cardboard, cut out the tracing, and mount the paper on it. That way the puppet will be much sturdier than if you used the paper all by itself.

A flat-sided stick has the advantage of offering a larger surface to stick things onto. You could make a very small stick puppet from a popsicle stick, a slightly larger one from a tongue depressor, and much larger ones from thin, flat scraps you might have lying around or be able to get for nothing from a lumber yard. As with spoon puppets, these stick puppets can be double-sided if you want to make them that way.

Paper plates come in different sizes and can easily be turned into faces, decorated with cotton or yarn hair around the edges. One on each side of a stick could give you two separate characters, or the same character with two different expressions. Instead of drawing in the faces, you could glue on buttons and scraps.

And what to do with them? A toddler may like to watch *you* make them move and talk, and then, later on, may want to do that for himself or herself. You'll probably find there comes a time when the best game seems to be for each of you to hold a puppet or two and, together, invent conversations or adventures for them. Children sometimes seem to need to be in control of *everything* that goes on in their play, but at other times they seem to like the unexpectedness of not knowing what another puppet may decide to say or do.

When Becky Galliucci was seven, she was fascinated by puppet play, and lots of them were stick puppets. One, I remember, had a picture of a toy soldier on one side of the stick and a picture of a tree on the other. Becky pretended her soldier was magic; whenever anything dangerous came his way, he just turned into the tree and whatever was dangerous went right on by.

Victor, her father, made her a stage. It was a three-sided affair—three frames of thin wood, each one nailed together at the corners, and all three tied together with string. The back and sides were as tall as the width of a roll of shelf paper. That way, Becky

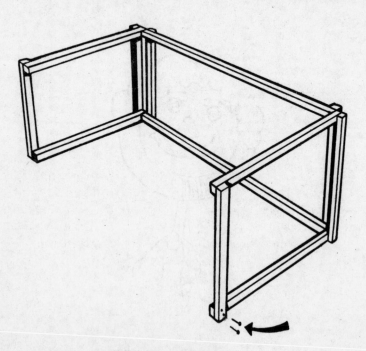

could make whatever backdrops she wanted and tape them to the inside of her stage. When we first saw the stage in action, it was placed on a table with the back sticking out about 3″ beyond the table's edge. Becky was under the table with her stick puppets, working them in the space between the edge of the table and the backdrop. As I recall, she made up a story about a fish family. She had done blue and green finger paintings on the shelf paper, and they looked like underwater scenes. Her fish puppets were all sorts of bright colors, some of which she had crayoned herself, and some she had cut out of magazines.

The next production we saw was staged differently. This time Becky was seated at a table pushed up against a full-length mirror. The stage was facing away from her so that you had to look into the mirror to see what was going on. We stood behind her as she took puppets out of her lap and worked them against the backdrop, but we could hardly see her hands moving . . . and anyway, we were all intent on what was happening on stage.

Using a mirror this way became Becky's favorite way of playing with her puppets because when she was alone, she could be both the puppeteer *and* the audience.

Though flat-sided sticks have their advantages, round ones, such as dowels, can work fine as well. If you have—or can get—a big square of pegboard, you might want to choose dowels that just fit into the holes. That way, you can move the puppets around from hole to hole. And what you put on the sticks doesn't have to be only puppets. You could put houses on them, or trees—in fact, anything you like that you make or find in pictures.

A pegboard like that could become a game of your own making. You could use a spinner, for instance (*see page 62*). You might paint sections of the pegboard the same colors that you have on the spinner, and a first spin would tell you in which section to place your puppet. A second spin would tell you which colored section was to be your goal . . . and how many holes in the board you could move in that direction.

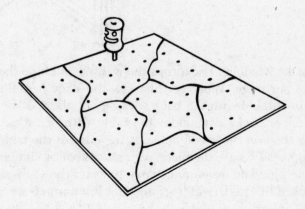

Or each section might have a different symbol on a stick—a house, a tree, an animal, or a car. Your game might be to visit each symbol and then get back to where you started. You could decide that your moves were over when you'd got back "home" again, and that your spins thereafter would go to the other player to help him or her get around the board as soon as possible.

We can imagine lots and lots of ways to play a game like that . . . with part of the fun being thinking them up.

PAPER-BAG PUPPETS Lunch or sandwich bags are conveniently hand-size. The way the bottom folds over lends itself to making a face and a mouth that moves. If you cut two holes in the bottom, you can stick your forefinger and middle finger through them and give your puppet wiggly ears.

BOX PUPPETS Small boxes (the kind that some puddings, gelatin, or single servings of cereal come in) can make puppets, too. If you opened them through a top flap, you'll want to tape it shut again. Then you can cut them around the middle on three sides. The folded fourth side becomes a "hinge" for the puppets' mouths. You'll see that your thumb will fit in the bottom half of the box and your fingers in the top half, and that they can make the mouth open and shut. The shape of the box you use will suggest where the puppets' features can go.

SOCK PUPPETS We particularly like sock puppets because they can take on so much character, and they're soft to stroke. If you pull a sock over your hand, you'll see that your knuckles fit right into the heel, while your fingers extend almost to the toe. You can take what's left beyond your fingers and tuck it back between your fingers and thumb, making a mouth that's capable of many different expressions. By the time you add buttons for eyes, material scraps for ears, and a tuft of cotton for hair, you'll have created a puppet that has real personality.

MARIONETTES Puppets on strings are usually too hard for young children to use, but if you have a floppy stuffed toy, you might want to try making a simple one. All you have to do is sew or tie on five strings—one to each foot, one to each arm, and one to the head. The other ends of the strings get tied to a length of stick or a cardboard tube. With a little practice, you'll be able to make the marionette walk, wave, and nod.

How children react to puppets says so much about how they're growing! To begin with, they may stay more interested in you than in the puppet you're working. There'll be a time when they get very curious about what's going on and how you're making it happen. They may look from you to the puppet and back again, over and over, until it all seems to make some sense. At some point they'll probably be able to engage in pretend conversations with the puppet, almost forgetting that you're there at all. Then, of course, they'll want to make the puppets move and talk themselves.

What children choose to say through their puppets is revealing, too. For a while they may find it easier to make their puppets say important things than to tell you those concerns directly. That may seem a safer way to try out talking about feelings. And depending on what they learn through those tryouts, they can come to feel at ease trusting you with their feelings, person to person.

When that happens, parents can really see how much their children have grown!

Some Other Ideas

You may have a supply of old clothes and hats to use for pretending, and that's a good use for clothing you're planning to discard. Here are some other ideas for dress-up that you can make from paper. They probably won't last very long, but the making of them can be fun.

MASKS Flat masks can be made from construction paper, but you might want to experiment with paper plates, too. They're roughly face-size, and they're sturdy as well.

Construction paper, though, is good for two-sided masks. You can make these by folding a large piece of construction paper in half and outlining the shape you want on one side, with the front of the shape running along the fold. For instance, if you chose to make a dog mask, it would be the dog's nose and muzzle that would be along the fold.

When you cut out your outline, you'll have two of the same shapes joined at the front. One shape goes on one side of your head, and one goes on the other. You'll need to make little holes in the parts of the mask that go behind your ears so that you can tie them together behind your head.

BEARD You can start with an ordinary piece of typing paper (8½″ × 11″). Leaving about a 2″ band across the top, cut the rest into a series of thin strips to make a fringe. You'll need to trim it to

fit your, or your child's, face. You can make the fringe long or short and any shape you want. If you'd like a curly beard, you can roll each strip in the fringe tightly around a pencil and then slip the pencil out of the roll.

Attaching the beard can be tricky. You can try a thin strip of double-sided tape, or several small pieces of tape that you've made into loops that are sticky all around. Tape may not hold very well, though, and can be irritating to a child's skin. Another possibility is to run a piece of ordinary masking or adhesive tape along the inside of the uncut band at the top of the beard (just to give the paper added strength), poke holes along the tape, thread a piece of string through the holes, and then tie the beard, knotting the string behind the head.

If you want a fluffy beard, you can spread a thin coat of glue over the fringe and stick on wisps of cotton from cotton balls.

MOUSTACHE   Stiff construction paper can make a fine moustache. All you have to do is draw, and then cut out, the shape and size you want. Taping it on may be a problem here, too, but you can try. An alternative is to cut a tiny triangle out of the middle of the top of the moustache—the part that's meant to go right under the nose. (The point of the triangle should be at the top of the paper.) That way, you'll have a sort of clip that can hold onto the part of the nose that divides the nostrils. You may want to leave the moustache just plain paper, or you could decide to stick wisps of cotton all over it the way we suggested for the beard.

CROWNS   Perhaps the easiest way to make crowns is to cut points along one edge of a wide band of paper that's long enough to fit around the wearer's head. You can use any kind of paper, even silver foil, and decorate your crowns with crayons or paint or glitter or anything you like.

You make a different kind of crown by pleating a large sheet of tissue or crepe paper and gluing one of the pleated edges along the length of a paper headband. When you've measured the headband to fit, and taped the ends together, you'll have a pleated cylinder. You can close the top of the cylinder by bending the pleated ends inward and gluing them to a cardboard disk 3″ or so across.

This kind of crown looks a little like a chef's hat . . . and being a chef is something you could pretend about, too.

ADMIRAL'S HAT   This is the traditional hat to make out of a sheet of newspaper, but if you have some sturdier paper you'll end up with a hat that will be more durable. Whatever you use, you'll need a sheet about 12″ × 18″ . . . which you then fold in half to make 12″ × 9″. Place the sheet so that the crease is away from you, and fold the upper corners inward so they meet at the center. You should now have two flaps at the bottom. Fold the top flap up, turn the hat over and do the same with the other flap. You'll probably need to tape these flaps in place, as well as taping the pointed front and back of the hat.

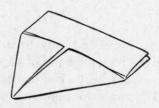

If you decide you want to paint these kinds of hats, spray paint is the easiest kind to use. It's important to avoid soaking the paper hat as you paint it, so two or three light coats is better than one heavy one. Each coat should be given time to dry before you apply the next.

Trimming the hat with gold braid or yarn can give it an added official flair, as can a jaunty plume. For the plume, you could use a large feather (if you have one or can find one), or you could make a plume by gluing cotton balls to the top half of a drinking straw and then gently fluffing them out into the shape you want. Because of the way the hat is folded, you'll find it easy to tuck the plume between the folds. A little glue will help hold it in place.

CRAZY HATS   By turning a medium-size paper bag inside out, leaving a turn-up on the outside, you'll have the basis for as crazy a hat as you care to make. It can be scrunched into any shape. You can draw loops of yarn around it, paint it, dab it with glue and stick scraps and buttons and just about anything else all over it.

SILLY SLIPPERS   To make soles for some paper slippers, try setting a pair of your child's shoes on a piece of construction paper and drawing around them with a felt-tip pen. When you cut out the drawaround, you'll have soles that are a little larger than your child's feet.

To make the tops for the slippers, set just the front half of the shoes on another piece of paper—another color if you like—and make two more drawarounds and cutouts. These second pieces will fit right on top of the insteps and toes of the first, and you can tape around the edges to hold them together. Your child's feet should be able to slip in between.

You and your child might want to draw toes on the slippers ... or faces ... or might like to paint them with glue and stick things all over them to make them silly. But your child might decide to leave them plain instead of fancy, and that's fine, too.

CHAPTER 7

THOUGHTS:
PLAY
&
FAIRNESS

As you watch children play, you can see again and again the beginnings of generosity and kindness and compassion and fairness. You can see the signs of consideration for another person's feelings. You can see little sacrifices being made to make someone else happier. You can see a willingness to wait for a turn on the trike . . . and a willingness to hand it over to the next person at the end of the turn. You can see a sharing of pebbles or marbles or toy cars.

Of course you can see the opposites, too. You can see dominance, manipulation, selfishness, ridicule and teasing, force and violence. Often you can see these darker sides of human personality in the very same children who at other times are quick to show the brighter sides.

It's certainly true that we all have our darker and brighter sides. No one is without both. I'm not aware of any explanation, though, of why it is that the darkness or brightness comes to dominate in a person's personality. Why is it that some people can keep their dark impulses under control, restricted to fantasy, and can even turn the dark energies they generate into bright pursuits?

Why is it that other people never do learn to control their dark sides?

Why, why, why? Sometimes "why" is as far as we can get. But whatever the answer and the cause, you can certainly see children trying out both sides of their human natures as they engage in play with their peers. I think the results of these tryouts, and the responses of loved adults who try to restore a sense of fairness when play gets out of hand, have a lot to do with whether a child's sense of fair play takes root and flourishes or not. I have known of children who, from infancy, grew up in emotionally deprived families where they were subject to consistent neglect and even abuse, families where there seemed to be almost no glimmer of caring or kindness. Yet, these children grew to be loving and compassionate adults and parents. Why?

I certainly don't claim to know why, but in my days as a student of children at play I so often saw how they were wrestling with feelings they couldn't control and, sometimes, couldn't even name. I saw, over time, how one child who came to the school angry and violent could, through play, learn to control his anger and violence and turn those angry feelings into angry paintings or pounded clay. I've seen, too, how, through play, a fearful child can learn to trust; or how a child who seemed to have no capacity for joy could slowly come to dance and laugh. Through play.

I don't think it's going too far to say that young children at play are taking what they've learned at home into an arena where they can try it out, and in doing so they are coming to their earliest understandings of "good" and "bad," "right" and "wrong." They are forming a system of ethics.

We asked Rena Galliucci if she could remember any incidents in the children's early years that stuck out as signs of the beginnings of "ethics." She thought for a while and laughed.

"There's always been one moment that puzzled me—and still does to this day. Stefano was five and Victor was three, and they were playing together in Victor's bedroom. I was passing by the door, and I heard Victor ask, 'Could God do that?' Stefano quite haughtily replied, 'Of course, silly. But he'd never be so naughty!' There was certainly some sense of ethics in there somewhere . . . and I'd give a lot to know what it was they were talking about!"

CHAPTER 8
ACTIVITIES: LOOKING & LISTENING

We're all explorers at heart, each in our own way, and the urge to find out about our world seems to come along with us at birth. How hard our eyes and ears and nose must be working during our earliest days as they try to make sense out of the countless new sights and sounds and smells that surround us! And how important our mouth is to us then, not only as a source of taste, but real *comfort.* By using our mouths we could make the inside ache of hunger stop. Our mouths could make noises, too, and those noises could bring someone to change us and make us more comfortable on the outside as well.

As we grew, our mouths started exploring our hands and fingers . . . and even feet and toes. Our mouths were probably exploring our caregivers' bodies, too—breasts and noses and cheeks and hands—and our caregivers were probably encouraging us to do so by giving us playful or affectionate kisses with *their* mouths. Before long we were able to control our hands a little . . . and we used them to bring just about anything we could lift up to and into our mouths for inspection. It was then that "taste" began to take on a life-long significance as a test of what was good to eat or bad to eat. Even then, the cautions and commands of our caregivers taught us much more about what should and should not go into our mouths than taste did.

As we learned that not everything could be explored by mouth, we began to rely more on our other organs and what they could tell us. And we learned to *remember*. That was truly a big step, because when we saw an apple again we didn't have to test it or ask about it as we did the first time. We already knew that it was good. Little by little, if we saw something with a "Mr. Yuk" sticker on it, we remembered that it was not for mouthing because we also remembered how upset our caregivers had been the first couple of times we touched something like that. We could probably remember the smell of cookies baking when we met that smell again, and it might make our mouths water in anticipation of something that *was* good to eat. That smell might even have led us to use our mouths to form a sound like "cookie."

Even the sound of the refrigerator door opening and closing might have alerted our mouths (and our stomachs!) to something good to eat coming our way because our eyes had told us very early on that the refrigerator was a place where lots of things that mouths could explore were kept.

As we grew, our other senses became the most important for our continued exploration of our world. In some ways, our hands replaced our mouths, our fingers telling us things about new objects that once our tongue had told us. Our other senses also began to protect our hands as they had our mouths at an earlier time. Our eyes and ears could tell us that a whirling fan might be dangerous to touch; our eyes and nose and skin could alert us that something was probably hot.

If we had something new in our hands and we didn't know what it was, then we'd bring it to the other senses for analysis. We might shake it and listen to the sound it made, or cautiously sniff it or taste it as our eyes told us as much as they could about the outside.

We must have done these sorts of things hundreds and hundreds of thousands of times in our early years, building up a store of knowledge and experience that became the foundation of our later understandings of our surroundings. I have no doubt that this foundation stays with us all life long and influences all our later searches for understanding and meaning. Fortunate children, I believe, learn from their caregivers in the very beginning that curiosity is good; that caution is necessary; that it's a source of joy as well as learning to look and listen carefully to what's around you; and that noting the similarities and differences in all that surrounds us is one of the best ways to appreciate the glorious diversity of creation and the uniqueness of ourselves. You'll know what kind of explorations your child is ready to undertake, but here's a variety of ways to go exploring—some of which you might like to try.

SHAPES & COLORS   The earliest explorations might just be journeys to discover shapes and colors. Your "explorer's kit" could be a notebook or sketch pad or piece of plain paper, and a box of crayons. The site of your exploration could be a single room in your house or apartment.

Whatever colors you can find in that room you can record on paper with the crayons. It doesn't matter what that record looks like—whether it's a single stroke, a scribble, a blotch, a patch or a dab. It's whatever you and your fellow explorer feel like putting down . . . so long as you can find that color in the room.

Before long, you'll probably have a lot of different colors all over the paper, and when you've recorded all the colors you feel like recording, you can start on shapes.

With a crayon that contrasts with the colors you've used (very dark usually works well), record the shapes you can find. Each time you find something round, you can make a circle somewhere on your color mosaic . . . and likewise for squares, rectangles, triangles, and plain-old straight lines. A window may have several shapes in it. Shelves, one on top of another, make interesting lines.

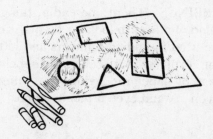

Is there a round clock face, or scroll in the arm or back of a chair? Is any of the furniture on little wheels? Are there patterns in any of the fabrics in the room?

You're likely to be surprised at what you begin to see in a room you thought you knew well. That's the way it almost always is when we shift our attention from the whole of something—like "the living room"—to all the tiny details that make up that whole. Learning to make that shift is a basic part of learning to look carefully and learning to see what there really is in front of our eyes.

Once you're done with your exploration, you can keep your creation of colors and shapes. It may have become sort of an "abstract impression" of the place you explored. You might want to label and date it. If it's on a loose piece of paper, it could be something to put in your scrapbook (*see page 42*), but you might find it interesting to devote a whole notebook to these kinds of explorations.

RUBBINGS   There's no end of things to look for, of course, and no end of places to look for them. As children get older, they'll be interested in finding numbers and letters and even simple words. Your "explorer's kit" can grow to include a magnifying glass, some sheets of paper for laying over things and then rubbing with a crayon . . . and even a picnic lunch.

What might you like to record on a walk around the neighborhood? If you found enough things for making rubbings, you could make a whole collage of them when you get home. There might be a variety of leaves and bark patterns to rub, metal insets in sidewalks, parts of manhole covers, plaques on the side of buildings, license plates, and probably many, many more possibilities that you'll have to look carefully to find.

If you're picnicking on a park bench, you might want to make an "abstract impression" of the area around you. What all can you see? How about writing down somewhere on the page some of the things you were eating at the time?

OUTSIDE SOUNDS   You could also add the sounds you hear to your abstract impressions. When you close your eyes, what can you identify? Some sounds you may want just to name—like car horns—but you may also be able to find word sounds to represent the noises. Instead of writing down "bird songs," for instance, you might come up with "ketch-a-cook, ketch-a-cook," or "tip, tip, tip, taree, taree!" Are there any machinery sounds around you for which you can find word sounds?

Wherever you're exploring, there will be sounds, and they'll certainly be different whether you're in the city or countryside, at a zoo or a construction site. Some of your explorations may be just for sounds, and a simple, battery-operated tape recorder can make a major addition to your explorer's kit. If you have one or can borrow one, you can set out to make sound collages to replay at home.

Some places you might want to explore are gas stations, laundromats, road constructions where there are jackhammers and backhoes, any place there's running water, a train station, bus station, airport, grocery stores, checkout counters, a park, a zoo . . . Is there a siren or whistle that goes off at noon? Or a town clock that strikes the hour?

INSIDE SOUNDS   Stopping to listen to the sounds of a house and the people in it usually brings surprises, too. We may find that there's much we hear that we take for granted but which, in fact, gives us a great deal of information.

Houses sound so different early in the morning, in the evening and late at night. To make inside explorations of the sounds around you, you really have to have a tape recorder because probably *you* are one of the chief sound makers—and the one your child listens for most carefully. If you're sitting quietly with your child listening for sounds, the house probably won't sound the way it usually does.

Can you find a way to capture fifteen or twenty minutes of before-breakfast sounds on a typical morning where you live?

How does that recording compare with before-supper sounds?

You may find that your child is curious about what sounds there are when he or she is sleeping . . . or even when all of you are asleep. If you have the kind of recorder that shuts off at the end of the tape, you could set it rolling when the last person in the family goes to bed. In the morning, you can try to guess what the sounds are.

Does it seem strange that the machine "heard" things that none of the rest of you did?

EAR TRUMPET   Just as a length of cardboard tube (from a roll of paper towel, perhaps) can make a fine mouth trumpet, so, too, it can make a "trumpet" to amplify sounds to the ear. Held against the microphone of a tape recorder, it will alter those sounds as well.

You might want to make several different kinds of ear trumpets and take them with you in your explorer's kit. You could take different lengths of cardboard tubing—from a toilet-tissue roll, a paper-towel roll, and a wrapping-paper roll. Do the different lengths make a difference in the way the sounds come through?

Can you find lengths of plastic or tin tubing to try out? How do they alter the sounds differently than the cardboard tubing? (Be sure to watch out for sharp edges!)

The shape of the ear trumpet will make a difference, too. You could roll a piece of heavy paper or light cardboard into a cone shape and listen through the smaller end. Do sounds come differently through a cone than through a tube? (Be sure the little end of the cone is large enough not to fit *into* the ear!)

Discovering Differences and Similarities

Explorations of any kind will give you many, many chances to compare things—to differentiate among sights, sounds, smells, textures, tastes, sizes, colors, shapes, and so on. But explorations also give you chances to talk about how things are alike. It takes a while for young children to become comfortable with the idea that things that are alike in some ways can, at the same time, be different in others. It takes time, too, for them to believe that you're not ever likely to find two things in nature that are *exactly* the same—not trees or flowers or blades of grass, not grains of sand or snowflakes, not shells, pebbles, or feathers.

Children's earliest attitudes to the fact of difference in nature probably stay with them as they grow and encounter more complex differences—in things, and above all, in people. It's here that children's early caregivers play such an important part in their growth. Whereas one caregiver might make a game out of trying to find two leaves that were exactly the same, another might make a game out of collecting leaves that were obviously different.

I can imagine the first game leading to a lot of frustration, disappointment, near misses . . . and the sense that there *ought* to be leaves that are the same. When I think of the second game, though, I can see a child scarcely older than a toddler running up to a parent, excitedly holding up two leaves and shouting, "Look how different *these* two are!"

There will be lots of times when you can pause for a moment to note differences, but you may want to balance those differences with similarities, too. All trees and leaves and plants need sunshine and water to grow, and all members of a species have some characteristics in common—characteristics that can be just as interesting to search for as are the differences. What's alike about maple leaves? Or sea shells?

As similarities and differences in simple things become easier for your child to notice and accept, you can extend their application to living creatures—dogs and cats and birds, animals in the zoo, fish in the aquarium. If you have an in-house aquarium with several fish of the same species, for instance, can you learn to tell them apart by tiny variations in their markings? But different as they are, they are all fish and they all need water and food and other kinds of care.

How about feelings? Can you tell how fish are feeling?

Your child may think so, pointing to a fish that swims "happily" up to the surface for food . . . or that stays "shyly" behind a rock . . . or that acts "frightened" when chased by a larger fish. However you may feel about fishes' feelings, you may be able to agree with your child that some animals make it easier than others for us to know how they feel.

For instance, can you both choose an animal you'd like to pretend to be and act out how that animal would be happy, sad, scared or angry? What might have happened to make them feel like that?

One day all this talk about difference and similarity is likely to get around to *people* and how each of us is like everyone else . . . and how each of us is unique. That, of course, can be the source of lots and lots of discussion over many years. Understanding the things that bind us together as human beings, and respecting them . . . well, that can be a lifelong task.

Understanding the things that separate us, one from another, and respecting them, too . . . well, that takes some people even longer.

One thing you can be almost certain about, though, is that as children become aware of and alert to the world around them, they will be very curious about human differences. Their early view of them may be quite different from your own. Sometimes they seem blind to ones that to us are the most obvious—as the following story suggests.

The father of a friend of ours was the white director of an all-black preschool. One day he and his preschoolers were out on a field trip on a bus. One of the black children said something to his seatmate that was derogatory about white people.

"Shhh!" said his friend. "Mr. Wylie is white, you know."

The first boy stared at his friend in disbelief. "He's *not* white!"

"He is too!" said his friend . . . at which point the boy got out of his seat and went up to Mr. Wylie and earnestly asked, "Mr. Wylie, you aren't *white*, are you?"

And I remember Rena Galliucci telling me about being on a bus with little Rita when she was four. Sitting in a seat across the aisle from them was a man with a misshapen ear.

"Momma, Momma!" shouted Rita, pointing. "Look at that funny ear!"

Well, of course the man heard and turned just as Rita was pointing, and it was an embarrassing moment for everyone.

"I told Rita that it wasn't nice to point at people if there was something unusual about them," Rena remembered. "I told her that it was fine to notice them and remember them, but that they were things we could talk about when we got home.

"Not long after, Rita and I were on a trolley where the seats faced each other. Opposite us was a woman whose nose was certainly larger than you might have expected, but it wasn't really anything that much out of the ordinary. Sure enough, though, the woman's nose caught Rita's eye. 'Momma, Momma!' she said at the top of her voice and staring right at the woman. 'There's a nose we'll have to talk about when we get home!' "

Exploring similarities and differences . . . that's certainly a part of looking and listening carefully. Here are some simple activities you might want to include in your play.

BUTTONS   A collection of buttons can be used for many things, but play with buttons does need care with very young children because buttons can so easily be swallowed. Buttons offer many chances to compare similarities and differences. After all, they're all buttons, but . . . there are round, square, and odd-shaped ones; wood, plastic, metal, and cloth ones; fancy ones and plain ones;

ones that have four holes or two holes or no holes; and they come in many different colors. You'll be able to find many ways to sort and compare them.

Flat buttons lend themselves well to games of tiddlywinks—trying to flip a button into a saucer by pressing on its edge with another button. The game becomes more difficult if you use a cup instead of a saucer.

Or you can play with buttons on a checkerboard, just moving them around any which way, or making up your own rules about moving and jumping.

You can play "Which hand?" with a button . . . or try balancing buttons on your forehead, nose, or the tips of your fingers. You could balance one on the back of your hand, toss it up and try to catch it in the palm of the same hand. You could try the same thing with two, three, or four buttons. How many can you catch this way?

You can even use buttons for buttoning. The next time you have an old shirt to make into rags, you might want to save the front strips—one with the buttons and one with the button holes. How many ways can you find to button the two strips together to make different shapes? You can use buttons for play money, too. Or your child might enjoy just starting a collection of buttons that you could display on a shelf. All sorts of surprising buttons turn up in thrift shops and yard sales, and if you find some that your child particularly likes, you could use them for real on a favorite shirt or coat. That can make an ordinary piece of clothing really special.

LAUNDRY SORTING   Any time when the family laundry gets done is a chance for a sorting and matching game.

How do you sort your laundry before doing it? Into whites and bright colors? Things that are delicate and things that are sturdier? Are there some things that need specially heavy-duty washing because of grease or mud?

The very same things are likely to get re-sorted differently when the wash is done and it's time to put the clothes away. There may be lots of different kinds of shirts, for instance, and even shirts of the same kind may come in big and little. How can you tell which pants belong to whom?

Can all the socks be paired up?

SANDING BLOCKS   The next time you pass a lumber yard, you might want to stop in and see if the managers will let you take away some of the scraps and trimmings—the little hand-size pieces that end up on the floor by the saw. A grocery bag full of them . . . and a couple of pieces of sandpaper . . . and you've got the makings of many hours of play.

While you're sanding off the rough edges, you can talk about the shapes and about rough and smooth. What else around the house is either one or the other? Can you think of rough and smooth things you might find outdoors? How about a lake or the ocean?

Someone might feel like painting the blocks different colors.

MATCHING KEYS   Lots of people seem to end up with a box of old keys that no longer have uses. If you've got a collection like

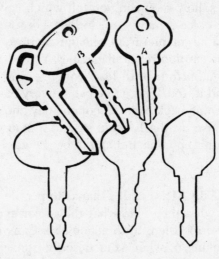

that, they're good for sorting, too. Are there long ones and short ones? Fat ones and skinny ones? Skeleton-type and Yale-type? How else could you decide to sort them?

If you take eight or ten of the keys and draw their outlines on a piece of paper, you'll have a puzzle that you can talk about: Which key fits which outline? What do you have to look for to find out? How hard this puzzle is depends on you and how similar are the keys that you choose. You might want to make it a little harder each time—if your child seems to enjoy the game.

HIDDEN OBJECTS   Forks and spoons from the same set are likely to have very similar, or even identical handles. When the other ends are hidden, it's hard to tell which is which—and you can make a little game out of trying to tell. Without your child seeing which is which, set a spoon and fork side by side and cover them with a sheet of paper towel. As you slowly slide the towel back to reveal the handles, little by little, how soon can your child tell which is the fork and which is the spoon? Is it any easier if the implements are turned face down?

If you have a sandbox (or feel like making one out of sand in a dishpan or deep-sided tray), you could bury the spoon and fork right up to the tips of their handles. By inching your fingers down the handles, how soon can you tell which is which?

Some objects may seem hidden because they're such small details in a larger picture. Calendar pictures might be good ones to use, or even pictures in magazines. You could take turns saying, "I spy . . . [a button? bird? leaf? watch?]" and see if the other person can find it, too. This game can be very easy or very hard. Rita Galliucci came back from school one day and asked her mother to find the snake on the Lincoln side of a penny. Try as she might, Rena couldn't find one and had to be shown. It was a copperhead.

SOMEONE IN MIND   It's thanks to people's differences in how they look, what they like, what they wear and what they do that we can describe them to someone else. Can your child guess who you're thinking of when your describe someone you both know? What clues seem to give it away? If your child is old enough to be the one to do the describing for you to guess, you may find it surprising what things about a person your child chooses as clues.

CARD SORTING   A pack of cards can be sorted many different ways. How many can you think up?

FAVORITE COLORS   Do you and your child have favorite colors? Are they the same or different? How many examples of the colors can you find by going through an old magazine? You could even cut out the examples you find and make them into a collage. You can decide whether you want to make two separate collages, if your favorites are different, or combine two colors into one collage. Are you finding different shades of the same color? Which are the lighter shades and which are the darker?

FAMILIES   When children start playing together, or start visiting at one another's houses, they soon become aware that not all families are the same. A child may suddenly become curious about someone else's family: "Jimmy says he's adopted. What's that mean?" Or curious about his or her own: "Why isn't there a daddy in our family?"

Whenever a chance offers itself, you may want to talk about the many kinds of families that children can have, from tight-knit family groups of several generations to the people who offer foster care. Children need to know that it's all right to have "different" kinds of families. They need to know, too, that the world is full of people who do care about children, and that all children need loving care from grown-ups. That's one way all children are alike.

LOTTOS   You can make a simple lotto game by cutting out one cardboard square about 2″ on a side and using it to trace around so that you have a dozen or so squares drawn on any large piece of paper or another piece of cardboard. (This will be your lotto board.) You may want to draw these squares in neat rows . . . or you may find it more fun to place them any which way. They just can't overlap, that's all.

Now you'll need two identical issues of a magazine that has pictures in it. Using your cardboard square, cut out anything you like that size, but cut the *same* things out of both magazines. That way, you'll have two sets of the same cutouts. Some of the cutouts might be objects you can recognize. Others might be parts of pictures that only make shapes. Still others might be blocks of printed words or a large capital letter.

One set of the cutouts gets glued down on the squares you drew on the paper. The other set gets shuffled up, and you can take turns drawing one and matching it to its mate stuck on the paper.

(You may want to mark the back of the cutouts with a big, black X so that your child can tell which side is the picture to look for. Or you may not want to if you decide to make the game a little more difficult.)

The next lotto works the same way as the first, but this time choose pictures that are similar but not identical. You might, for instance, stick down a picture of a clock and cut out a picture of a wristwatch as its matching partner. Or you might pair up a shoe and a boot.

For the third lotto, you could choose two things that in some way have to do with one another but are very different. You could take a horse and a saddle, say, or a car and a gas pump—whatever you can think up from the pictures you have handy.

And here's another alternative: you can take one big picture and cut it up into six or seven puzzle-type pieces that have distinct shapes. Then, you can trace around these shapes on another piece of paper so that when each piece is matched with its shape, the picture is whole again. If that seems too easy after a while, you can see if your child can assemble the picture without the help of the outlines.

Lottos and puzzles were very popular with several of the Galliucci children when they were growing up. Victor Sr., luckily, enjoyed thinking up more and more variations as the years went by. He enjoyed the cut-and-paste work, too. He recalls making an elaborate lotto game for Becky for, he thinks, her sixth birthday. There were about thirty pictures stuck down on a piece of thin plywood, and the pieces for matching were mounted on stiff cardboard. He didn't make the matching easy, either.

"I've forgotten a lot of what went into it now," Victor told us, "but I know it took me quite a time to think them all up. There were several word plays, I recall. I had a picture of the head of an elephant, and its mate was a picture of the kind of trunk you pack things in. And there was a picture of the rein on a bridle of a horse and rain on a window . . . and, oh yes, a clothes hanger and an airplane hangar. That took Becky a long time to get. There was a snapshot of me and a picture of a balloon bursting. 'Pop' is what she always called me.

"One square was completely blue, and that went with a picture of a blueberry. And there was a picture of Yul Brynner to be matched with another of a wig. It wasn't meant to be a game to sit down and do in five minutes, as you can tell, and I don't think Becky finished it completely for maybe two months. What was fun was that the matchings went off like little time capsules. She woke Rena and me very early one morning shouting through the door, 'I got one, Pop! I got one!' Another time she had to call me at the motel where I was staying on a business trip.

"When she was all done, she made all of her friends guess and guess and guess. She could be so scornful of their efforts, and I had to remind her several times that she hadn't always known all the answers, either! The best thing about it was that it was such fun— for all of us!"

ACTIVITIES: LOOKING & LISTENING   **125**

Musical Instruments

Music has been important to me since my early childhood. Why it becomes more important to some children than to others is hard to say, but for me it has been one of the best ways I can express my feelings for as long as I can remember.

You don't need to be a musician, or even musically gifted, to find pleasure in playing with sounds. All children naturally do so, even hearing-impaired children for whom sounds take the form of vibrations. In fact, my experience with people who are hearing-impaired has taught me that we all *feel* sounds far more than we realize.

A child's first experiences of "music" may be the musicality of a mother's voice as she speaks in the particular lilting way that parents have when they're talking to their infants. A child's own cooing is musical, too. Little by little, children come to learn that these cooing sounds come from within themselves . . . that they can imitate other sounds they hear . . . that they can control the sounds they make . . . and that they can use these sounds to tell people things. (Sometimes, much later on in life, that may turn into opera!)

Children, of course, aren't aware that all these steps are happening, but when you think about it, it's an amazing kind of growth that's taking place.

The awareness of rhythm comes early, too. Infants, when they're lying on their backs and drumming their heels on the floor, are making and feeling rhythms. There's rhythm in all the talk that infants hear around them, in the songs of birds and even in the sounds of traffic. There comes to be rhythm in the ways young children use their bodies. (Sometimes *that* turns into dance!)

Encouraging children to play with sounds and rhythms leads to all sorts of pleasures and useful outcomes. One, certainly, is helping children learn to listen carefully. Here are some things you and your child might like to make together. Whether you think of them as noise makers, rhythm makers, or musical instruments is up to you.

HANDS   They're always with us . . . and they can be a source of endless rhythm patterns and several different sounds. Can your child repeat a simple clapping rhythm that you make up? How about a more complicated one? What happens if your child is the one to make up the rhythm, and you're the one to copy it?

You could show your child the different sounds hands make when they're cupped and when they're stretched flat . . . and when, instead of being clapped together, they're patted on other parts of the body.

How many people in your family can snap their fingers?

CHEEKS   Flicking a finger against your cheek will produce a variety of sounds depending on how much your mouth is open and how much you purse your lips. It's even quite easy to play a simple tune on your cheek. If your child knows "Mary Had a Little Lamb," for instance, you might try playing that one.

VOICE   Our voices are among the best and most versatile instruments of all. You could make a game with your child out of singing high and low, loudly and softly. You could try singing into cupped hands and while holding your nose. And of course you can add words and even make up simple songs of your own.

HORNS   Cardboard tubes of any size can make horns to hum or sing or talk or shout through. If you like, you can punch some holes in the top (or glue on buttons) to make pretend finger stops. If it's summer and you have a garden hose lying around, that can become a long, long horn to hum through. A person can even hum in one end and listen at the other at the same time.

GUITARS   Rubber bands stretched around lidless boxes make guitarlike instruments. The depth of the box and the length and

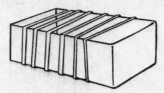

thickness of the rubber bands will all make a difference in what kinds of sounds come out.

DRUMS Just about anything can be a drum . . . and that can turn into a problem that may need you to set some limits! Drums offer a good chance for you to help your child practice self-control. Soft is just as important as loud, slow as important as fast. Your child might like to try drumming along with some music, too, even trying to keep a steady beat to the music's rhythm.

CHIMES You can make chimes from spoons by hanging four or five of different sizes from a stick—a string around each handle and the scoops hanging down. When you hit the hanging spoons with another one, you'll find they make different sounds depending on their size and what they're made of.

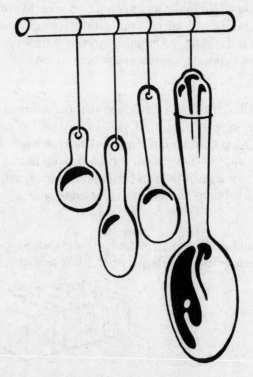

BASS FIDDLES Plastic containers of all sizes are useful for these instruments. They can be margarine-size, yogurt-size, or much bigger. What you need to do is poke a tiny hole in the bottom of the container and thread a length of fairly hard, fine cord through it. About a 3′ length will generally do. Then you tie the end of the cord that's inside the container to a piece of popsicle stick or anything else that will stop the cord pulling back out of the hole. You can tie the other end around the middle of a popsicle stick as well so that you'll have something to hold on to. Then you can set the container upside down on a bare floor, rest your feet lightly on it, pull the string tight, and pluck it. You won't be able to get a *lot* of different notes, but depending on how tight you're pulling the string, they will come out higher or lower in pitch.

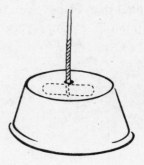

BLOCKS Knocking two blocks together makes another rhythm sound, and you'll find that hardwood blocks make sounds that are different from softwood blocks. You might also want to cover one side of each block with a piece of sandpaper cut to size. You can then alternate knocking sounds with scraping sounds.

MARACAS Two paper plates, glued together and partly filled with dried beans, rice, or unpopped popcorn, can be another addition to your rhythm section. Of course what you choose to fill them with will determine how they sound when you shake them around.

WATER MUSIC   A glass container partially filled with water will give off a musical tone when you tap it with the side of a spoon. Some containers ring better than others, and how high or low the note is depends on how much water you put inside. You can try a selection of sturdy glasses or jars and see what kinds of notes you get. If you feel ambitious, you can try to put together a number of containers that will give out the notes you need for a simple tune—for instance, "My Country 'Tis of Thee."

(You'll find you can also get musical tones by blowing across the top of empty bottles. Adding water to the bottles will alter these tones as well.)

GONGS   Any small sheet of metal, a brass platter or even a cookie tin (lid, bottom, or the whole thing) will give off a gonglike sound. What you hit it with is up to you . . . and depends on how much of a racket you want to make. If you want a sound that is more muffled than clangy, you could try wrapping the scoop of a wooden spoon in several layers of cloth and tying the cloth tight.

You'll want to find a way to hang your gong from a string; holding it will dampen the sound and make it more drumlike. If you end up with a gong that appeals to you, you could hang it somewhere in the kitchen and use it to tell everyone when dinner is ready.

Some Other Ideas

MUSICAL DESIGNS   This art project, though intentional, relies on spontaneity; you don't want to think ahead too much about what you're going to do.

You can use any materials you like, from pencils to finger paint, and choose any piece of music, familiar or not. The idea is to listen to the music and just let yourself loose on a large piece of paper, making whatever marks in whatever colors the music seems to suggest to you.

Young children are likely to have trouble at first understanding relationships among listening, feeling and doing; they may tend to get so absorbed in their painting that they stop really listening to the music at all. It can be helpful for you to say how the music is making you feel, for instance, "That part's making me feel purple and wavy. Now it's becoming yellow and sharp!" Try to use these comments as reminders and encouragement only, though. You may find it helpful to add, "How does it make *you* feel?"

The point, after all, is for each of you to come up with something different, and for your child to feel that there's no correct or incorrect interpretation, only interpretations that are uniquely his or hers.

STRING PAINTINGS   Expressions of creativity are sometimes accidental. (Even when the product seems accidental, though, the *process* is usually intentional.) Here's an example where the product is always a surprise:

Take a piece of paper and fold it in half. Crease it and open it up again. Dip a foot-long piece of string in any color of nontoxic

paint and arrange it in a squiggle on one half of the paper, leaving a little piece of the end hanging off the edge. Fold the other half of the paper over onto the string. Press firmly on the "string sand- wich" as you pull on the little end you left sticking out.

That's the basic process. You may want to repeat it several times on the same piece of paper, each time using a contrasting color and turning the paper around so that you're pulling the string in different directions. Whether or not you let the paint dry between pulls will make a difference you may find interesting, and the kind of paper you use—plain white, or colored construction— will produce different effects as well.

Do the shapes and colors you end up with suggest any images? Some people find it fun to add *intentionally* to the final product with crayons or colored markers.

CAMOUFLAGE   The English word "camouflage" comes from Italian and French words that mean "to disguise." When some- thing is camouflaged, it usually means that it's hard to see because it looks like something else. Camouflage is useful when you want to hide.

You can play a simple "camouflage" or "hiding" game with a

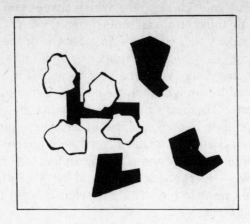

young child by cutting a simple shape or letter out of one color of paper and gluing it on a sheet of contrasting color—for instance, pasting a red T on a white background. The T, of course, will be easy to see.

The picture changes, though, if you tear or cut pieces of the leftover red paper and stick them here and there all over the white background. Because of its shape, you'll still be able to see the T, but the eye will have to work a little harder to isolate it from the background.

Can your child still find the T?

You can make it harder still by tearing up pieces of white paper and sticking them on the T itself, even across the T's edges so that they break up the straight lines. When you're done, you may find that it would be hard to guess there was a T to begin with.

You could make another camouflage game out of scraps of wallpaper or wrapping paper.

For instance, you could cut out a circle, a triangle and a square; or a couple of numbers and letters; or even the shape of an animal . . . whatever you like. As you move your cutouts around on a sheet of the same paper, do they suddenly seem to get "hidden"?

You could actually stick several of these shapes onto a larger piece (without your child seeing which shapes you're using) and tape the whole thing on a wall some distance away. Can your child see all the shapes you used? How close does he or she have to come to find the last one? If you use rubber cement and rubber-cement remover for this game, you'll be able to play it again and again.

Older children might like to know something about camouflage in nature. There are little green worms that live on green leaves . . . and they're hard for birds to see. There's the chameleon lizard that can change its color to blend with the color of what it's lying on. There are many animals you can find at the zoo that rely on camouflage—tigers and leopards and black panthers.

If people want to hide at night, what colored clothes would they choose to wear?

If you were playing hide-and-seek in the woods, how would you dress if you didn't want to be seen? What colors would you avoid?

INVISIBLE PICTURES   Soap can act like a crayon, but if you use white soap on white paper, you won't be able to see the marks you make—at least, at first. You can use the corner of a soap bar for drawing, or you can cut a thick slice off the bar if your child finds that easier to hold.

To make the marks appear, you can rub over them with a soft lead pencil. Rubbing with the *side* of the point works the best.

You might want to make simple squiggles to begin with. You could also try a letter or a shape. After making a few of these invisible pictures together, you and your child might find it fun to make surprise pictures for one another, each doing the soaping out of sight of the other. If your child can read and write, you can even give each other surprise messages.

SAND DRAWINGS   Any flat surface with edges will do as a "canvas" for this activity—a serving tray, cookie sheet, cake pan or box lid. Basically, the idea is to sprinkle a thin layer of sand over the flat surface, drawing in it with a popsicle stick, a pencil eraser, finger or the like. Shaking the "canvas" will, of course, erase the design or picture, and you can start again. (Salt or cornmeal can be an alternative to sand.)

If you have a large box lid that you can use, you can begin by painting the inside surface with several bright colors of nontoxic paint. It doesn't matter how you paint it; it could be in strips or splotches or patterns of any kind. The lid does need to be thoroughly dry, though, before you add the sand. Now, when you draw in it, your lines and shapes will seem to turn different colors as you go.

Another variation is to start by drawing with glue—the kind that you can squeeze out of a nozzle or apply with a brush. As soon as you've applied the glue, sprinkle the sand over the whole thing and give the glue time to dry. Then shake off the excess sand and see what you've made. If you want to go further, you can color the unsanded sections. You can also add to the creation by gluing on pieces of yarn and fabric, beans, popcorn (popped or unpopped), buttons, or anything else that's at hand.

SKIMMERS   Round cardboard disks can be made to skim through the air by cutting a pie-shaped wedge out of them. (You can draw a neat circle on your cardboard by tracing around the lid of a saucepan. When you cut it out, the circle doesn't have to be perfect in order to fly.) You can try skimming with small disks and large ones, varying the size of the wedge you cut out as well. For starters, you might want to try a disk about 10″ across and cut out a wedge that's about 2″ wide at the rim.

Painting your skimmers several bright colors can be fun because they'll look quite different in flight than at rest. Any designs will do.

PENDULUM GAMES   Playing "catch" takes a lot of coordination. For a toddler, even rolling a ball back and forth with someone means anticipation and timing; control over muscles in the arm, hand and fingers; the measurement of distances and direction by the eye; and a brain that's developed enough to synchronize the whole act. "Catch," of course, involves skills that are a lot more complex yet.

Nonetheless, "catch" seems to be a favorite game for parents and their growing children. This version makes it a little easier.

The idea is to make a long pendulum that swings back and forth between the two players. What you'll need is an eye screw, a length of string, and a weight. The eye screw might go into the lintel of a doorway, a ceiling beam, or anywhere else up high where you don't mind making a small hole. The string should be long enough to reach to the floor. One of the best weights we've seen was a homemade bean bag (*see page 30*) filled with gravel. (Sand would be fine, too, but you'd want to seal it in a plastic bag before putting it in the bean bag.)

When one end of the string is attached to the eye screw and the other to the weight, the pendulum should swing clear of the floor by two or three inches. That way, your child can stand at one end of the pendulum's path and you can sit on the floor at the other end and play "catch." One advantage of this contraption is that when someone misses, no one has to go chasing a ball!

This game can evolve into another one by placing an object right where the weight hangs when it's hanging straight down. The goal is to knock the object over. The thinner the object, the more difficult the game will be. An empty pop can, for instance, will be quite easy; a candle (in a flat, unbreakable candle holder) will be more difficult. And the game will be more difficult still if you place the target object to one side or the other of the pendulum's lowest point.

One family turned this idea into a yard game. Their pendulum was fixed to the limb of a tree about 10' off the ground. Perpendicular to the pendulum's path they'd placed a long board, and along the board they put a variety of targets. They had different-size, empty detergent bottles and a couple cans, all ranged according to size, with the largest targets at the outsides. Right in the middle they put a candle stub that was just tall enough to knock over. The way they placed the game, the outside targets, though tallest, were the hardest to hit, and so they counted more points. As the players got more and more skillful at the game, they had to stand back farther, and this tended to even out the advantage that frequent players had over first-timers, or that grown-ups had over children.

Sometimes they played partners—a grown-up and a child on each side. It became a popular family pastime and the source of healthy, good-natured competition.

CHAPTER 9

THOUGHTS: PLAY & AUTHORITY

Once children start playing together, you may find them experimenting with all sorts of approaches to authority. For instance, who's going to decide who chooses the game or makes up the rules? Who gets to say, "You be the mommy," or "You're it"?

Who settles the squabbles?

"You already had a turn!"

"I did not!"

"You did so!"

Often it's the oldest who gets these roles, just because he or she *is* the oldest. Seniority, even at that age, has a way of counting. But sometimes it's the bossiest who makes the decisions . . . or the one whose yard the play is in . . . and sometimes, to an adult watcher's surprise, children actually take turns being the boss and being the bossed.

And how does the boss carry his or her authority?

"You've got to do it 'cause I said so!" (And that's an order!)

Or: "You've got to do it 'cause that's what the rules are!" (It's company policy!)

"The game won't work if you don't do it!" (We're all team players in this division!)

Or: "If you don't do it, I'm gonna tell my mommy!" (I'll report you to your supervisor!)

Or: "I don't want to play with you anymore!" (You're fired!)

Some children seem naturally more comfortable with one style than with another. Some, as they grow older, can shift from one to another to see which will work best. Some can give in more easily than others and come up with "Okay, we'll do it *your* way this time."

How and why do children *resist* authority? What provokes an "It's not fair!" or an "I don't want to!"? Under pressure from the boss to continue playing against his or her will, a child might go mute and curl up with a comforting thumb or a blanket, might go find a comforting adult, might knock over the block structure under construction, might wallop his or her playmate. What lessons do you suppose children learn as they try out these various responses?

There is so much to observe as children sort out their pecking orders and arrange their play patterns. You may find yourself smiling sometimes to catch in their play such clear parodies of the adult, the "real," world. But, if we could know the truth of the matter, I suspect it would be the other way around. Far from their mirroring our world, it is we who are continuing to act out, in our adult "parodies," the games and responses we all first learned in childhood.

Adult structures in work and play didn't just suddenly appear, full-blown, when we grew up. Whatever takes place in the adult world has its origins in the childhood we all went through. It may look very different in size, scope, or degree—whether it's welfare, the World Trade Center or war—but it's nothing new. That shouldn't be too surprising, because that's the way it is with each of us as well. However we look or act or feel today reflects even our earliest times in this world. No matter how much our outside selves may change, they still enclose, within, the infants, children and teenagers we once were and will always be.

Trees tell me these things are so. When I look at a mature tree, can I see the sapling it once was? Is it still there? Is this a different tree than was the sapling? Yes, different but still the same.

CHAPTER 10
ACTIVITIES: TAKING A JOURNEY

Victor Galliucci tells us that his family had a favorite game he played with all his children as they were growing up:

WALLA WALLA   "We called it 'Away to Walla Walla' because we liked the way that sounded. For us, Walla Walla was a place where anything could happen. We could get there anyway we wanted to and come back any time. Over the years, the children found lots of ways to use Walla Walla. I remember watching five-year-old Rita teaching Becky to play peek-a-boo when Becky was all of eighteen months old. Instead of saying, 'Peek-a-boo!' Rita was saying, 'Away to Walla Walla!' when she covered her face with her hands, and 'Home again!' when she uncovered her face.

"The different children used Walla Walla in different ways at different times," Victor went on. "For Victor Jr., it was a place we used for bedtime stories. I remember a time when four-year-old Stefano built something that looked like a fortress out of blocks and called it Walla Walla. No one was allowed to touch it. Rita had her mother put a blanket over a table in her bedroom so that she had a private place to crawl into. That was *her* Walla Walla when *she* was four. She's fourteen now, and just the other day, when she was telling me about someone she thought was a little out of touch with reality, she said, 'You know, Dad, sometimes I think he's kind of in Walla Walla!' "

As I listened to Victor, it sounded as if he and his family had used Walla Walla in many of the same ways that we use the Neighborhood of Make-Believe in *Mister Rogers' Neighborhood*—as a place for pretending and magic, a place that could help clarify the difference between reality and fantasy. But there was also lots in what Victor remembered about Walla Walla that had to do with going away and coming back, with practicing about leaving and returning, with being away from someone you loved and then getting back together with them again.

We've mentioned that theme of separation several times and that's because it's such an important one for young children to work on through play! If we could go back to our earliest experiences with small separations, we'd probably find the beginnings of our later feelings about big separations—the ones we're all faced with as we and the people we love grow older. Little by little we have to learn to comfort ourselves during the times we can't be with our loved ones, and as we do so we are developing the inner resources to move us through even the grief of a death into new times of joy.

It may seem strange to talk about death and a game of peek-a-boo in almost the same breath, but perhaps the idea that tiny separations help us get ready for bigger ones will make putting the two together seem a little less odd. Have you noticed how solemn a baby can become when you cover your face with your hands? It's almost as if you'd actually gone away. And the sudden delight when you take your hands away again? You've come back!

It's not until children are into their second year or so that they can understand that something they can't see can still be there. Before then, you may find that your child won't even look for a little toy he or she has been playing with if you put a cup or a cloth over it. It's gone, that's all.

When you leave the room, you're "gone," too, and there are times when your leaving may cause an outburst of real distress.

But as you come back again each time you say you will, your child can learn to expect you back, accept temporary care from others, and find things to do during the waiting times when you are away.

How much can you remember about your early separations from the people you loved? Perhaps the first ones you can remember are times when you were homesick at camp or somewhere else where you spent nights away with people you didn't know very well. When you think back, can you pinpoint the time when you "left home" for good to be out on your own? How did that feel? Recalling some of those times is a good way to get closer to the feelings about separation your child may be dealing with.

Separation, of course, is a two-way street, and for some parents it can be very hard to be away from their children. I've known of mothers who couldn't bear to be separated from their young children at all—who took them everywhere with them, who never left them with a baby-sitter, and who came to dread the first day of school. I always wonder what such mothers' own early experiences with separation were like. As they work through their feelings now about being away from their children, though, they will have another chance to come to terms with the anxieties that may be leftover from their own childhoods. That's an example of the way our children give us another chance to go on growing.

You don't, of course, need a Walla Walla—or a Neighborhood of Make-Believe—for play about going away and coming back, but you may find that having an imaginary place to go can help the play get started.

Deciding Where Walla Walla Is

We asked Rena and Victor Galliucci whether each of their children had one particular place that they used as Walla Walla—such as the block fortress and the table covered by the blanket. But as they tried to remember how it had been, it seemed clear that the children's Walla Wallas had been wherever they'd wanted them to be at the time of their pretending. Rena remembered going to Walla Walla with a child under a tree in the backyard; in a corner of the back porch; behind the sofa in the living room; in the garage; and, naturally, in the children's bedrooms.

"Just about anywhere," Rena concluded after thinking about it. "One summer we went to Walla Walla for a while every day under an umbrella on the beach. And that reminds me: whenever we'd take a long trip in the car, someone would always go to Walla Walla just by closing their eyes! When a couple of the kids would go together, it was always fun to listen to their adventures—all the things they pretended to see and do. Strange, but I don't think I ever remember a fight breaking out in Walla Walla. Not even between Victor Jr. and Rita, who never seemed able to get along for five minutes with their eyes open. I wonder why that was. Walla Walla always seemed big enough for everyone's pretend."

Getting There

Victor Jr. was back from college the other day, and we got talking to him about what he remembered of Walla Walla. Interestingly enough, his most vivid memories were not of Walla Walla itself, but of the adventures he and the others would make up about trying to get there.

"I guess when I was very young, like maybe four or five, Dad and I would be in Walla Walla just by saying we were there. And then we'd think up funny things to do. I don't remember a whole lot about what we did, but I do remember being with him, particularly snuggling up close to him on the back porch during rainstorms in the summer. I'd've been much too scared to be out there alone! Anyway, if there was thunder and lightning, we'd pretend that we were making them happen. We had one gesture for lightning—snapping open your fist as fast as you could, sort of like you were flicking water at something. You had to guess, just kind of *feel* when the lightning was going to flash. It was amazing when you guessed right and the flash went off right when you told it to, like you really made it happen. And then we'd guess when the thunder would follow and make-believe we were beating on tom-toms.

"But like I was saying, what I remember most was making up adventures about getting to Walla Walla. Those have got to have gone on right up to the time I started junior high. We'd pretend to set off in boats and planes and spaceships, and we'd always have a lot of accidents and disasters. The boat would sink and we'd have to float off somewhere in a raft, or the plane would crash-land in the mountains and we'd have to survive in the snow and ice ... you know, that kind of thing. Lots of times that ended up being most of the game. As soon as we reached Walla Walla we'd start off again on a trip home ... and for some reason, that trip was always safe and sound. Lots of times we'd pretend that there was a ticker-tape parade or a band to greet us—not to mention Mom and the rest of the family!"

As we listened to Victor, it occurred to us that there are lots of things you could do about getting to Walla Walla.

SUITCASE   This project is quite an undertaking, and you may prefer to turn a sturdy, ready-made cardboard box into a suitcase. Many families have enjoyed working their way through the steps that follow, though. For them, the pleasures of working together made the effort worthwhile.

How thick a weight of cardboard you use for this suitcase-from-scratch depends on how durable you want it to be. If it's really going to be used for carrying things around, or even taking things for an overnight visit, then you'll want to find cardboard that is good and stiff, such as the corrugated kind. It will be harder to work with, but it will be worth the effort.

You'll need two sheets of cardboard—one for the bottom and one for the top. Bear in mind that the suitcase will be about 5" or so smaller all around than the size of the sheets you choose.

The first thing to do—on the sheet you're going to make the bottom of the suitcase—is to score the cardboard from side to side and top to bottom about 5" or so in from the edges. (How far in you choose to make the score marks will determine how *deep* your suitcase will be.) You'll do that all around: four times. When you've finished, you should have a 5" square marked at each corner of the sheet.

(A note on scoring: scoring means making an indent in the cardboard so that it will fold more neatly and easily. With heavy paper or thin cardboard, you can usually score with a blunt knife. With heavy or corrugated cardboard, though, you will need a sharp edge, and you will actually have to cut about halfway

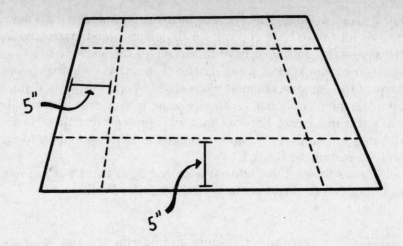

5"

5"

through the cardboard to make it bend and fold. It's a good idea to tape over any of these cuts when you're done or they may soon wear through.)

With any side of the sheet facing you, cut the side of the little square that's on your right. Just that one side.

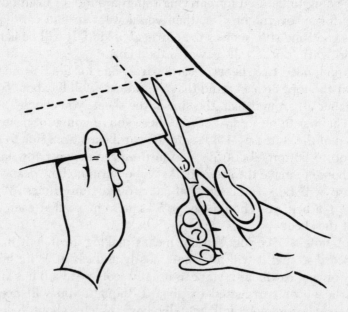

Now rotate the cardboard clockwise and do the same thing . . . and again . . . and again. Each of the four squares should have one side that's cut when you're done.

The next thing to do is to turn the sheet over and fold each side up along the score marks you first made. You'll see then what those cuts were for. They've given you tabs to fold around at each corner of the box to hold it together.

The tabs have to be fastened in place, of course, and you may want to glue them. You can also tape them with strong packing tape or duct tape. You might even want to run a length of tape clear around the box you've made. Best of all might be to glue the tabs first, and then run a piece of tape around so that the tape will help hold the tabs in place while the glue dries, as well as help give the suitcase extra strength.

So much for the bottom.

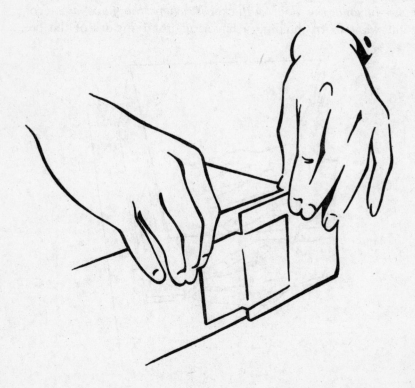

The top needs to be just a little bit larger than the bottom and about 2″ deep. You can save yourself some cutting by using two outside edges of the second sheet of cardboard, but first draw lines 2″ in from those outside edges. You'll need that margin to make the flaps that fold down.

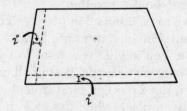

Now you can turn the bottom upside down and trace around it, putting *one* of the long sides right along one of the lines you've drawn, *but leaving an extra 1/4″ to 1/2″ around the other three sides—beyond the double thickness where the flaps are.* (You might want to try holding a finger against the sides of the box

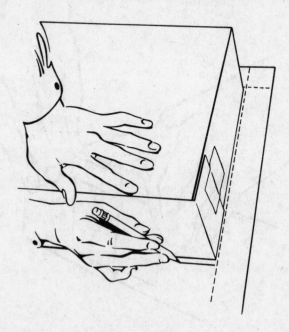

while you're doing the tracing; that may give you just the extra leeway you need.)

Once you've got the basic outline, you'll need to continue the 2″ margin around the remaining two sides.

Before you go any further, it's best to cut out this larger shape and score all the lines you've made for easy folding. What you have now is something very similar to the shape you had when you were making the bottom, but this one has smaller squares marked at each corner, and the cutting will be a little different.

With either of the long sides facing you, cut out the squares to your right and left—not just one side of the squares this time, but the whole thing. You'll be left with a long flap, and that will become your *hinge* flap at the back of the suitcase. (We'll get to how you attach it in a moment.)

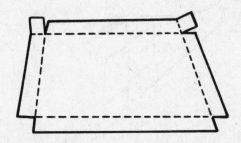

Now rotate the sheet clockwise, and cut only the *side* of the square to your right. Rotate once more and do the same thing again. Now you can turn the cardboard over and fold all the sides up along the score marks, even the hinge flap. This time you'll only have two tabs to fold around the front corners, and just as before, you can glue them in place, tape them, or both.

With any luck, you'll find the top fits comfortably over the bottom. If it doesn't, well, you'll have the chance for some real talk about disappointment, patience, and the willingness we all need from time to time to try something again until we get it right!

But let's say it does . . .

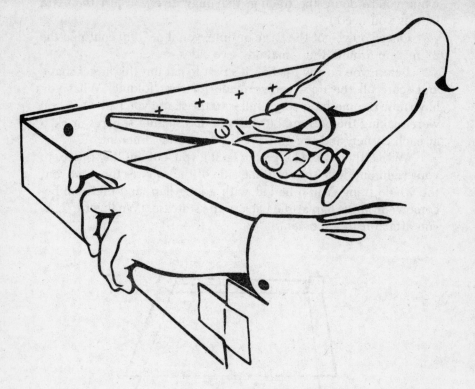

Now's the time to attach the hinge flap. We suggest you put the top in place and then poke good-size holes every 2″ or so along the flap and through both the flap and the side of the suitcase bottom. (The line of holes can run along the center of the flap or, perhaps even better, a little closer to the fold of the hinge. If you're using heavy cardboard, you may want to poke through the flap first, then mark through the holes with a pencil onto the suitcase bottom, and then poke through the pencil marks.)

You'll need a long piece of strong string (or cord) to tie the two together, and you can use the same technique we suggested for binding the scrapbook (*see page 43*). Just push the string through the first hole at either end of the line and pull it to its mid-point; thread either end back and forth through the holes; do the same with the other end, threading it through the holes in the opposite direction so that you're making a series of figure 8s. It

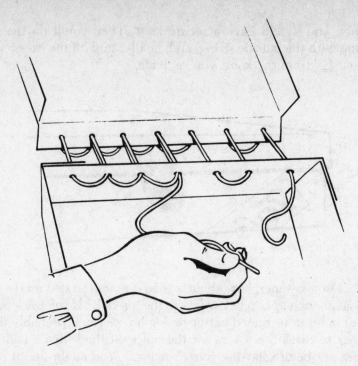

doesn't matter how loosely you do the threading at the time, but when you're done, pull it all good and tight.

You're now left with one end of the string on the inside of the suitcase and one on the outside. Holding the outside one tight, take the inside one and tuck it under the string that's coming from the last hole . . . then back over that string and under itself . . . and pull tight (making a half hitch). If you repeat this three or four

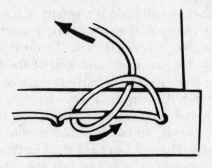

times, you should have a secure knot. Then you'll do the same thing with the outside string; and, finally, snip off the excess string about ½" from the knots you've made.

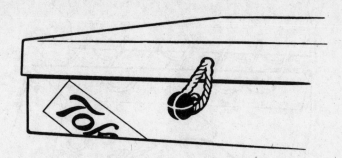

For a fastener, how about a good-size button tied on the front about an inch or two below where the top falls? If you use a button with holes in it, they'd better be *big* holes. You'll probably find it easier to mark the places for the holes on the suitcase and poke them out before starting your "sewing." (You might find it easier still to use the kind of button that doesn't have holes but has a little "handle" on the back.)

Once you have the button in place, you can poke a hole in the suitcase's top, right above the button. Then you can thread a loop of bright yarn through the hole from the inside, and when you've found out how big the loop has to be to go over the button, you can tie the inside strands into a knot that's too big to pass out through the hole.

The last thing you'll need is a handle of some sort. You could attach an old drawer pull if you have one around. If not, you could make a handle out of braided yarn. To do this, you'd begin by poking holes where you want each end of the handle to be, and then threading three lengths of yarn through one of the holes and knotting them together on the inside. Holding the three strands side by side, put one of the outside strands over the middle one . . . then the other outside strand over the middle one . . . back and forth, back and forth until you have the length of braid you want. Then put the unbraided ends through the other hole and knot them together on the inside, too.

Once you have the suitcase made, you can discuss how to decorate it . . . and what you want to pack in it to take to Walla Walla or anywhere else you decide to go for real or pretend.

MAKE A PICNIC You could, for instance, make a pretend picnic and pretend to eat it when you get to Walla Walla, or you could really pack up some special snacks to take with you.

TRANSPORTATION If you have some straight-backed chairs, you could put two or three in a line, one behind the other, and call the chairs whatever kind of transportation you like. Who's going to be the driver or the pilot?

TICKETS & MONEY Dollar-bill-size pieces of paper are fine for paper money, and if you want some small change, pennies, buttons, paper clips, shells, pebbles (or what have you) will do.

If you think you'd like to make your paper money look more official and important, why not stamp it with a potato print? You can do this by cutting a raw potato in half; carving any design you like into one of the flat faces; pressing the carved face into an ink pad, or into a few brushstrokes of poster paint or finger paint. If you have some vegetable coloring on hand, that will work, too. (You might want to try printing with other hard, raw vegetables such as halved onions and carrot tops.)

As for tickets, you can make them out of just about anything. Any narrow strip of thin cardboard or heavy paper about 3″ long can make a ticket. You can collect colorful ones from box tops—rice boxes, cereal boxes and the like.

On the way to your "transportation," you could pretend to stop by the ticket office and take turns selling tickets to each other.

Where would you like to go? (You certainly don't *have* to go to Walla Walla!)

How would you like to get there? Quickly or slowly? (You could turn the chairs into donkeys and go that way.)

When do you plan to come back? Today? Tomorrow? Whenever you feel like it? Do you need a return ticket as well as one to get you there?

Does anyone else want to come along? A doll or teddy bear? Several? Does someone have to stay home and wait for you to come back?

How much do the tickets cost? Have you enough money?

Have you any baggage to put on board?

When does the "transportation" leave? Right away? After a while? In five minutes? (You could set a kitchen timer, get aboard, and do some waiting until it rings.)

Are there seat belts that need fastening?

How much you want to make of the journey is up to you. It might be a quick trip . . . or a long one. It could be such a long one that you'd have to pretend to eat and even sleep on the way.

The more your traveling companion can decide about these things, the better. The older that children get, the more decisions they're likely to feel able to make—and the longer they'll be able to sustain this kind of pretend. As I've watched people working with children at play, and through the times I've done so myself, I've become aware of what a knack it is to catch the rhythm of children's play at different ages—just as it is to fit in with their changing moods from day to day. (There's also the knack of being able to bow out of their play once children seem to be carrying it out on their own!)

As adults, we tend to make a plan for the things we do, and then we try to follow it so that we can get to a particular outcome. When we're going somewhere new, we like to have maps. To get done what we have to do, we like to have date books and schedules. When we get lost, or our timetables go awry, we can feel very frustrated and upset. It's easy for adults to bring this kind of viewpoint to children's play, but when we do, we're likely to find that the play doesn't go very well.

Young children's play may often seem random and illogical. For no apparent reason, some character in a child's fantasy play may suddenly decide to go to work, or may get sick, or feel hungry or sad. All at once, a house may be on fire, or, just after a whole family of dolls has gone to bed, they may decide it's time to go for a ride in a car. I believe we need to try to avoid the temptation to straighten out the time sequences and practicality of children's play ideas. They come from somewhere—of that we can be quite certain—and they have a logic of their own and their own meaning. Most likely, they reflect feelings that are surfacing inside, one leading to another, each breaking through in a different image or story line. We can be most helpful when we gently coax these feelings into words and allow them to take their own forms. That's one way we can support the development of our children's creative imagination and their ability to express their feelings in the ways that come most naturally to them.

What's important is that our children do find ways to express what's going on inside their minds and bodies. Often we may just have to accept what they say or do without really understanding it. You might find it interesting (and often amusing) to jot down some of the images that your child comes up with as you play together.

Here's one Rena Galliucci noted that came from Becky when she was four:

BECKY: (*pointing to a milk-carton house*): That one's on fire!

RENA: What happened? How did it start?

BECKY: Somebody was playing with matches.

RENA: Is there anyone in the house?

BECKY: (*shakes her head*)

RENA: Can the firemen come?

BECKY: Nope.

RENA: Why not?

BECKY: They're at the zoo.

RENA: At the zoo? Is there a fire at the zoo?

BECKY: (*shakes her head*)

RENA: Then why are they at the zoo?

BECKY: They're having a picnic. Then they're going swimming.

Things to Do in Walla Walla

You may already have your own ideas about what to do in Walla Walla, and that's what it's for: a place to do whatever you feel like doing and to pretend whatever you feel like pretending. Here are a few ideas, though—ideas you can do anytime and anywhere.

HIDING GAMES The simplest "hiding" game is probably peek-a-boo. It's such an old form of play and one that I'd expect to turn up, in different forms, in cultures all over the world. I say that because all children face some of the same developmental tasks as they grow to know who and what they are.

Playing peek-a-boo is one playful way of learning that something that's hidden for a time can still be there. It can go away, but it can come back, too. When what's hidden is the face of someone you love, it's *really* important to learn that it's still there and can come back.

When a young child is the one in the game to hide his or her eyes, something similar—but different—is happening. That child is learning that when we hide or close our eyes, the world and the people in it don't disappear or go away; we can count on everything's being there when we open your eyes again. Getting this kind of reassurance may be very helpful for some children who seem anxious or even fearful at bedtime. Night brings a long separation, and it's one that can be hard for small children to manage until they have come to feel sure that everything—including you—will still be in place come morning.

You could play about bedtime in Walla Walla. You could pretend to go to sleep, or your child might want to play the part of the grown-up and put you to bed, acting out any family rituals you may have as you get ready to go to sleep. As you play the part of the child, you might pretend that you want to stay up just a little bit longer . . . or want a glass of water. When you stall like this, what does your child do about it? You might ask your child to let you know when it's time to wake up. How long does he or she let you "sleep"? What happens if you pretend that you want to sleep a little bit more?

One way to get an idea of how well your child understands about things that are hidden is to play a simple game with three or four small objects such as a stone, a stick, a leaf, and a flower. When you're sure your child knows what they are, you can line them up, ask your child to hide his or her eyes, and then cover one with a handkerchief. Which one is hidden? Where has it gone? Of course, if your child is a little older, you can actually take one of the objects away and hide it nearby, perhaps saying "getting warm" (when your child moves toward it) and "getting cold" (when he or she moves away from it).

You can take the idea behind peek-a-boo a step further by hiding under a blanket yourself . . . and then popping your head out. What does your child do when you are hidden?

As in all these games, children's reactions depend on their understandings of what's going on. If you stay under the blanket for more than a moment or two, a child, up until a year old or so, may be solemn or even alarmed to tears to find you suddenly "gone." By toddlerhood, your child will probably be eagerly stumbling into you or crawling over you, full of the pleasure of knowing that you're still under the blanket even though you're out of sight. Soon after, your child may enjoy being the one under the blanket—but only after he or she has come to feel sure that you're still going to be there upon looking out from under the blanket again.

A little later still, you could change the game so that you slip off and hide while your child is under the blanket—but you'd best let your child know ahead of time that that's what's going to happen. Don't be surprised even then if you find your child somewhat uncertain about what's happened when you're not right there where you were. Soon, though, most children will come to feel secure that you can be somewhere else than where you were . . . but still close by. With that understanding in place, the fun of real hide-and-seek can begin.

You're likely to find, too, that by the time a child can play hide-and-seek, he or she is also feeling comfortable with your going away from the house for a while. That's not exactly hide-and-seek, of course, because the "hiding" lasts longer and your child can't come running after you to find out where you've gone. But the same knowledge that you're out there *somewhere* can help him or her cope with your time apart—that, plus the reassuring knowledge that you *will* come back again because that's what you've always done before.

TAG STORIES   Tag stories are stories that one person starts, another adds to, and so on, until someone makes the story end. If there are just two of you, of course, you'll take turns back and forth adding to the story line. Additions to the story can be any length you like, from a single sentence on up, and no one says that they have to make grown-up sense! It can be interesting to see what children come up with at different ages, and you might want to make some of your additions have to do with some character going away, or with something getting lost. What additions does your child feel like making to that sort of story line?

TELEPHONE CALLS . . . AND A TELEPHONE   Once you're "away" in Walla Walla, you might find a time to talk about the people you left behind. Is there anybody particular you'd like to have had along on the trip? Where do you suppose that person is right now? What do you suppose that person is doing? If you felt like it, you could give the people you're thinking about a pretend phone call. You could ask them how things are going with them and tell them where you are and what you're seeing and doing in Walla Walla.

You don't need any "telephone" for this kind of pretend; you can just hold your hand to your ear. You might enjoy making one, though. Here's one way to do it . . . along with what it led to for the Galliuccis and the Warninskis.

The two families share a primitive summer cabin out in the hills an hour east of town—a cabin that has no electricity and, naturally, no phone. For the two sets of parents, it was a relief to get away from a jangling phone. They all work and they have a busy social life, too. But for the children, some of whom were just developing acute cases of "telephonitis," it was hard to be out of touch with their friends even for two days. And unless they could get an invitation to stay the weekend in town with another family, they had to go to the cabin because they were still too young to stay at home by themselves.

Fortunately, with several children in both families, there was plenty of companionship. All the same, Martha Warninski remembers, one or other of the children always seemed to be complaining, "Can't we get a phone out here?"

Frank Warninski, who was eleven, seemed to be the worst complainer of all, so, for a birthday joke, his mother decided to make him a toy telephone.

She took the cardboard tube from an empty roll of toilet tissue and painted it bright enamel red. That's what she used for the handle of the earpiece. Then she found two good-size pine cones and painted them beige. Because of the way pine cones grow, she

found she could wedge them into the ends of the tube—one to listen to and one to talk into. (The pointed parts of the cones fitted into the ends of the tube, and the flat bottoms stuck out at just about the right angle.) To keep the cones secure, she dabbed some glue right where the cones and the tube touched.

Then she decided she needed a cradle for the earpiece. After looking around for a while, she settled on a plastic cottage cheese tub. She turned it upside down (leaving the lid on) and cut out the bottom. Once that was done, she cut out two half-circle scoops in the sides, one right opposite the other. She made them just big enough for the toilet tissue tube to rest in. She painted this base with flat white paint, and when it had dried, she repainted it a glossy black and filled it with small pebbles to make it heavy and solid. For the final touch, she attached the earpiece and the base with a piece of string.

For the Warninskis and Galliuccis, this telephone—or "telecone" as they came to call it—took on a life of its own, a life that began one April Fools' Day. Stefano was by then seventeen and had chosen to stay home rather than go to the cabin, but he gave a pre-recorded tape and cassette player to Victor Jr. to take out with him. The tape began with several telephone rings, after which Stefano had recorded his side of an imaginary telephone conversation with his father. Victor Jr. turned it on just as everyone was sitting down to supper at the cabin. When the phone started ringing, he said, "I'll get it!" and then, "It's for you, Dad . . ."

After that first experiment, they all thought up lots of ways to make "telecone" conversations!

SENDING LETTERS Another way people stay in touch when they're away, of course, is through the mail. Your child is probably aware of the mail that comes to your house and may be curious about how it gets to you from distant places.

You could pretend, in Walla Walla, to send someone a letter . . . but you could also send a real one. What have you been doing or seeing, or pretending to do and see? Your letter might go to someone else in the family, or you might find it fun to send a letter to each other, keeping the contents secret from one another until they're delivered. Your child's "letter" to you might be just a scribble or a drawing, or, perhaps, a rubbing for you to guess what it was made from. (If your child needs help getting it into an envelope, the chances are you can do so with your eyes closed so that it *will* be a surprise.) Once you've stamped and addressed the letters, you may be able to think up an adventure to take you to the mailbox. You might, for instance, pretend to be looking for a secret door in a castle.

As for how letters *really* get from place to place—you could take a trip to your nearest post office one day and talk about how real people move letters by hand, in vans and on airplanes. If your visit to the post office happens during a time that isn't a busy one for the people who work there, someone might be able to show your child how letters are sorted so that they get to the right houses.

Some Other Ideas

NONSENSE   Words are wonderful toys, and as soon as children begin acquiring them, they begin playing with them in different combinations. A three-year-old and his father were putting a puzzle together one day and the boy decided he wanted to try by himself. "Me do it all by my lone," he said. That was a sort of nonsense, but it made good sense all the same.

Making nonsense rhymes often gives very young children delight. If you take the lead, you may find your child gladly following. "I know what color that is," you might say. "It's purple-skerpel-merpel-ferpel." Pointing to another color, you might ask, "What color is that?"

Sometimes children's nonsense words are versions of what they hear—the closest they can get. "Breakfast" may become something like "beckwist," or a sandwich may become a "sammitch." Other times, though, it may be impossible to know what the word means at all. A three-year-old, looking at an ink-blot picture, said that it was a "wufftingle." "Can you tell me more about a wufftingle?" asked the grown-up who was with her. The girl shook her head. That's all it was: a wufftingle.

It's tempting to correct children as they begin picking up words, to help them get things "right." While we certainly need to help them learn the words and structures they need to express themselves, it's worth trying to keep that learning both light and fun. The enjoyment of language leads naturally to puns and riddles, to nonsense verse and, quite possibly, to the appreciation of more serious prose and poetry later on.

The Galliuccis often played word games to pass the miles on long journeys in the car. We asked Victor to recall some for us.

"One favorite," he told us, "was a game I'd played with my family when I was little. It was called Hink Pink. Actually, it was introduced to us by my mother's sister from California. She was our 'Auntie Mame' and would suddenly turn up in her RV—land yacht, she called it—on her way from one place we'd never heard of to another. Anyway, if you said you had a Hink Pink, that meant you'd thought of two one-syllable words that rhymed . . . and you had to give a clue as to what they were. For instance, you'd say: 'I've got a Hink Pink and it's a brightly colored sleeping place.' The answer would be 'red bed.'

"I think our kids were getting the idea of Hink Pink by the time they were four or so, although the structure of the game wasn't entirely clear to them. They'd say things like, 'I've got one! A fog log!' That was the first sign they were catching on, and just by listening to the rest of us, they began understanding what a 'clue' was and that the answer was for other people to guess.

"You could have a Hinky Pinky, too. That meant each word had two syllables. And even Hinkety Pinketies of three syllables. The answers tended to get sillier and sillier the longer we played. Somebody came up with a Hinky Pinky that was 'a catapult for flower holders.' That turned out to be a 'fling-pot slingshot.' Our all-time favorite was a Hinkety Pinkety that Rita, my wife, came up with. It was 'a tandem kitchen utensil.' The answer? 'A two-seater eggbeater.'

"We also played a game called Exzoobits. That was a word that meant 'exhibits in the zoo.' For instance, you'd say: 'If you and your mother were walking through a really smelly place, what exzoobit—exhibit in the zoo—might you mention? In that case, the answer was 'Pew!, Ma.' Get it? A puma. I remember Stefano asking me: 'Dad, if you were seeing me off on a plane, what exzoobit might you mention?' His answer was, 'Bye, Son'—a bison. Exzoobits, let me tell you, weren't easy to find and got pretty silly at times. In our opinion, the sillier they were, the better!"

BIRDFEEDER Sometimes when you're out for a walk in the neighborhood or in the park, you might want to make a point of looking for birds. How many different colors can you see on the birds you find?

This would be a good time to collect pine cones to bring home, too, because they can make birdfeeders to hang outside your windows. All you have to do is to tie a long string around one end of a pine cone, smear peanut butter into all the grooves and hollows, and roll the whole thing in bird seed or sunflower seeds.

When the birds come to your feeder, are some of them the same kind you saw on your walk? Are there new ones as well— ones with other colors?

Where do birds go at night? What kinds of journeys do they take in winter?

WALL HANGING Wide masking tape hanging from any kind of rod forms the basis for this wall hanging. You might want your

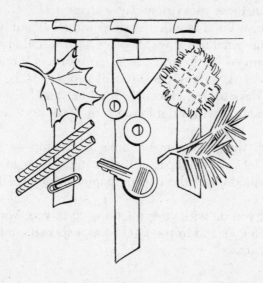

hanging to have just one single strip, or you might want it to have several of the same, or different, lengths.

Once you have your strip (or strips) in place, you can cover the sticky side with just about anything you like, provided the objects aren't too heavy. Things you find on your journeys outdoors make good hangings—leaves, sticks, grass, pebbles, even horse chestnuts. If you felt like it, you could make each strip of tape into a souvenir of one such outing.

What sorts of things can you find around the house to make an *indoor* hanging?

PIÑATA   In Mexico and Central America, children usually make piñatas at holiday times. (You might want to locate these places on a map. How would a person get there?) They're papier-mâché shapes that are hollow inside, and parents fill them with little toys, sweets, and other surprises.

To make a simple piñata, you can start by blowing up a balloon and tying it shut. Next, tear up some newspaper into lots of thin strips, soak the strips in diluted paste, and stick them onto the outside of the balloon until it is completely covered. To make the piñata sturdy enough to hold things, you'll probably need five or six layers of these sticky newspaper strips.

If you've left a length of string on the balloon, you'll be able to hang the piñata in a warm place to dry. Otherwise, you can bend a strip of cardboard into a more-or-less circular stand on which to set it. In any case, it will probably take the piñata a couple of days to dry. Once it's dried out and hard to the touch, you can paint it with bright colors, or decorate it any other way you want.

To fill the piñata, cut a hole in the top—a hole just big enough to let your hand pass through. In doing so, of course, you'll pop the balloon, but the outside papier-mâché shell will remain intact.

What you do with your piñata is up to you. You might want to keep it on a stand in the kitchen as a special container for nutritious treats.

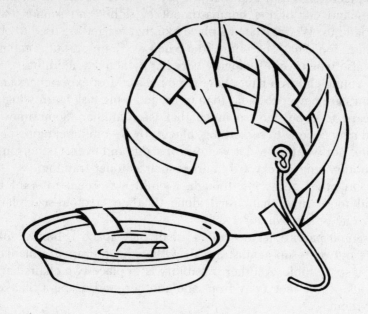

In Mexico and Central America, though, blindfolded children try to hit the hanging piñata with sticks until they break it open and make the contents fall out. If you want to try this game, you could bend a wire coat hanger so that the "shoulders" fit down through the hole and spread out inside, while the hook pokes up through the hole for tying onto a piece of string. That way, if you wanted to, you'd be able to hang the piñata from something like the branch of a tree.

One piñata we saw was used this way at a birthday party. After the cake and ice cream, everyone went out into the backyard to help the blindfolded birthday child try to whack the piñata and let loose the party favors that filled it. All the guests stood back and shouted, "Left!" or "Right!" or "Higher!" or "Lower!" until, with a resounding smack, out came a shower of little toys for everyone to play with.

PRIVATE PLACE   Most of us have felt the need for a quiet, private place to go now and then—a place where we can be by ourselves and out of the bombardment of sights and sounds that surround us. We may need a place like that for getting used to our feelings, too. That's certainly true when we're upset, but it can be true also when we're suddenly very happy about something.

Young children have these same needs. Most experiences and feelings are newer to them than to us, and a big task in growing is to learn to cope with so much that is unfamiliar. Sometimes a child may cope with something difficult by becoming clinging and whiny, not wanting to let you out of sight, and even taking some temporary steps backward in areas such as toilet training.

On other occasions, though, a child may seem to want to spend more time than usual alone. Is there a child-size place where he or she can go?

Some parents have made a small play space behind a sofa that's not quite up against a wall. Others have draped a blanket over a spare table. Another possibility is to place two chairs back to back, a few feet away from one another, and drape a blanket over them.

Whatever the space you can create in your home, it needs to be small and cozy. If you have a cushion or two to put in it, along with a couple of favorite books, perhaps a flashlight, and some little toys, so much the better.

Above all, children need to know that such spaces *are* private, their own, and that you understand their need to have them.

CHAPTER 11

THOUGHTS: PLAY, CAUSE & EFFECT

One more block makes the tower tumble . . . a little more water makes the pail overflow . . . swinging a bat around can hurt someone . . . tracking mud through the living room can make people angry . . .

The things I do make other things happen.

That sounds so simple, but what a breakthrough in understanding it really is! From the awareness that things don't "just happen," and that it isn't only grown-ups who make things happen, comes a child's gradual feelings of power, mastery and control. Those feelings grow slowly, and as they unfold, they reveal some unexpected fruits.

One, for instance, is that wishing and pretending do *not* make things happen: not good things and not bad things, either. Wishing can't change the weather or make us grow faster. Some things are beyond the control even of grown-ups, but things like that have reasons why they happen, too, even though the reasons may be hard to understand. And pretending is just make-believe: we can pretend that we are different, or that life is different, we can try out how we think it would feel to be a bus driver or a dancer, but at the end of our make-believe we're still going to be who we are. If we really want to be different in some way, we're going to have to do something about it, not just pretend.

It must have been exciting when we first realized that if there was something we wanted to have happen, we could often make it happen—or at least help make it happen. Of course we also had to learn that there were some things that neither we nor anybody else could ever make happen no matter how much we might want to. We might really want to be able to fly all by ourselves . . . but that's not something we can really do—we can only pretend about it.

We also had to learn that as much as our growing mastery and control let us make good things happen, they also let us make bad things happen. What's more, we *did* make bad things happen from time to time. That may have been scary because we probably believed (to begin with) that doing something bad could make a loved grown-up stop loving us. It may have been so scary, in fact, that we may have needed an imaginary friend for a while to help us—a friend who could take the rap for the muddy tracks in the living room, the broken vase or the spilled milk. We may have had to spend a lot of time playing out breaking things and scolding people, or scolding our animals or our dolls. Perhaps it was by being "really mad" at a doll that we also came to realize that we still loved that doll. With that realization may have come, in turn, an inkling that the people who were really mad at us could still go on loving us as well.

Knowing that our actions have consequences isn't always easy to face. It can be still harder to take the responsibility for sad or unfortunate consequences we may not even have foreseen.

The things I do make other things happen.

With that awareness comes both joy and pain, and it turns out not to be so simple after all.

CHAPTER 12

ACTIVITIES: AROUND THE NEIGHBORHOOD

Just about everything a very young child does adds to his or her knowledge of the world and how the world works. There are things that are soft and things that are hard, things that taste good and things that don't, things that make noises of different kinds and things that fit together in different ways. A baby playing with a rattle is a person who is learning with eyes and ears and mouth and hands.

Learning, at that age, is automatic. A baby doesn't have to *try* to learn; everything, being new, has something to teach, and the young and growing mind stores up these lessons as they come along. In seemingly no time at all, a baby "knows" more things than we could possibly count, and soon begins the gradual process of learning words and meanings and names and colors and shapes and uses. There's no end to it, of course. As long as we live the more we learn . . . and the more there is to know.

The suggestions for activities in this chapter are offered as ways to help children expand their awareness, curiosity and understanding of many everyday things that they're likely to see around them. There's as much to learn from the making of the things we suggest as there is in the playing with them. And they can be played with in any way a child chooses. To us, a tunnel may be a tunnel, but the one we describe could just as well be turned upside down and become a bathtub for a doll. For a particular child at a particular time, feelings about bathtubs might be much more important to play out.

We've imagined the construction of a play neighborhood with some of the elements you'd be likely to find where you live. You certainly don't need to follow the sequence of activities in the order we've written them; we just had to begin somewhere, and one idea seemed to lead to another. And we don't really expect many people to build a whole neighborhood because we know most families would be hard put to find enough space. See what appeals to you and make of our suggestions whatever you like.

ROADS   It can all begin with a simple crossroads: eight pieces of masking tape stuck down on any open space such as a porch or floor. If you picture how the sidewalks at an intersection come together in corners, you'll see the shape we have in mind—two pieces of tape to make each corner, with the roads running in between.

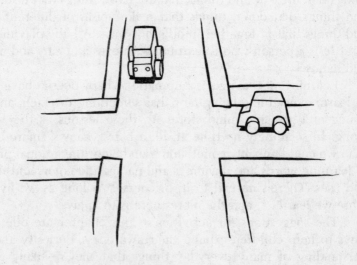

You may find that even a simple shape like that holds a surprising amount of interest for a child. There are borders that suggest limits, and there are directions and choices to try out. With a little push car, or just a block that can be an imaginary car, you can go in from one side, turn up or down, circle around the outside, come in from another direction and go straight through . . . or zoom across the tapes any which way.

You can use two "cars" and see what happens when they go in the same or different directions, or make up a race . . . and cause collisions. It can be a game to play alone, or one to play with someone else. If you happen to be the someone else, a child may enjoy giving you instructions about which way the cars should go and what they should do. It's a chance for a child to be in charge of someone else for a change—in charge of someone who usually makes those kinds of decisions.

Being in control of pretend situations comes out again and again in children's play, and you'll probably see it many times and in many different forms as you and your child play together. You're also likely to find times when your child wants *you* to take charge. It's reassuring to children to know that the adults in their lives are really in control and are always available to take over when situations get beyond the comfortable limits of their own abilities to cope.

Your child might want to extend the arms of this crossroads so that the roads continue—straight, or zigzagging, or turning corners, or joining in other crossroads. Soon, you may have quite a maze of routes to move through. Where do they lead? Where are the people in the cars going?

VEHICLES   It was Stefano Galliucci who came across the following way to make a variety of vehicles out of egg cartons. He was fifteen at the time, and he remembers his younger brothers and sisters pestering him to make them "by the dozen." What his mother, Rena, remembers best about them is the awful noise they made when she stepped on them. "And that was pretty often," Rena said, "because for a while they seemed to be *everywhere*! I can hear that sudden crunching sound now, and it gave me an

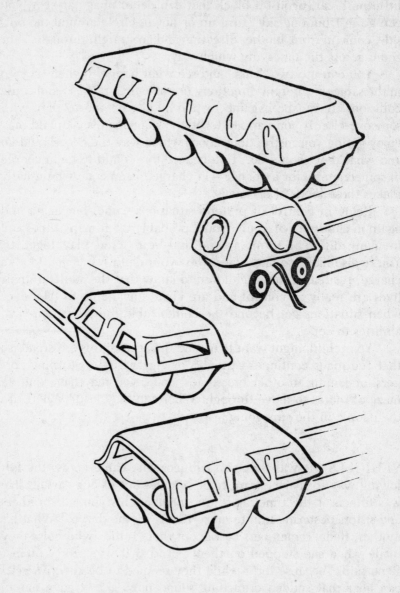

awful start each time it happened. And if it turned out to be one of the kids' favorites . . . well, you can just imagine the uproar!"

Stefano's basic vehicle was a four-seater, and he started by cutting off the end of one of those styrofoam egg cartons. He cut it crossways so that there were four little wells and a hinge on one side that let the top swing open and shut.

Next, he cut out the side panels and back panel to make windows, and he even went so far as to glue clear plastic wrap over the inside of the windows and across the opening in front so that his car had a windshield. He poked slits in the sides of the passenger wells and threaded garbage-bag twists through them to make seatbelts for his passengers. With another twist, he made a door latch to keep the top shut when he wanted it to stay that way.

Finally, he took a thick magic marker and drew shapes that looked like headlights on the front, brake lights on the back, and spoked wheels on the sides.

The one he made for us slid along the carpet or floor just fine. It had a space-age look—sort of an all-terrain vehicle you might expect to find exploring the surface of the moon. He said that he and his brothers and sisters had painted a lot of them silver and red and other bright colors, and that they'd had fun doing the painting, too.

To make busses, he'd just made six- to twelve-seaters instead of four-seater "cars." And he'd also made neat little two-seaters, which they pretended were motorcycles. These opened on a hinge front-to-back. They didn't have much stability all by themselves, but Stefano solved that problem by poking slits in the side and, again with garbage bag twists, giving each motorcycle a kickstand. After that they worked just fine.

It sounded to us like these egg-carton vehicles could be just about anything you like, depending on how big they were and how you wanted to decorate them. They could be mail vans, ambulances, school busses, police cars, or fire trucks.

RIVER & BRIDGES   The simplest "river" we can think of is a long strip of blue cloth. You may have something old and blue lying around, but if you don't, you can always take something old and white and dye it with vegetable coloring. That can be an interesting project in itself. Of course there's no rule that says a river has to be blue, either. In fact, rivers around the world have been named for just about every color of the rainbow. You might want to ask your child: "What color would you like the river to be?"

Your river can flow anywhere you like—on the outskirts of the roads you've made or right across some of them. Either way, you may need some bridges. You can make good bridges out of cardboard cylinders by cutting them in half lengthways and then cutting off the amount of bridge you need. Little bridges can come out of the tubes found in toilet tissue or paper towel rolls. We found oatmeal cereal containers an easier size to work with.

To give these bridges better stability, we suggest you score lines on both sides of the cardboard ¾" or so in from either side of the bridge. You can fold these tabs inward or outward and tape them to the floor, or set them on strips of double-sided tape. (We

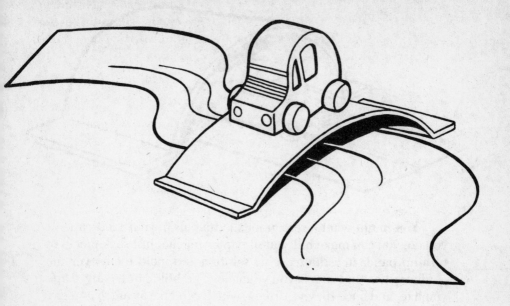

don't recommend using thumbtacks because they have a way of working themselves loose and hurting everyone around.)

Some people have made these same kinds of bridges out of tin cans, and there are many sizes to choose from. They're harder to work with, though, unless you have tin snips, and you have to be *very* careful to make sure that all sharp edges are smoothed out or taped over.

TUNNEL   What works as a bridge can also work as a tunnel. If one road goes through while another goes over, then a single cardboard arch can be both bridge and tunnel at the same time.

"Under," "over" and "through" are playful words! You can certainly go under a bridge, but can you go under a tunnel? Do we go over bridges, or do we really go over rivers? Of course we could fly over a bridge, too. Can we go over tunnels? We can go through tunnels, that's for sure. Are there times when we can go through bridges? How about covered bridges or draw bridges?

You might want a reason for the tunnels in your landscape. If you do, you can make hills out of papier-mâché. Just soak pieces of torn-up paper in a diluted glue solution and mold them over the cardboard or tin tunnels you've made. The hills can be any shape you like, and once they've dried—which can take as much as a day or two—you can paint them if you choose.

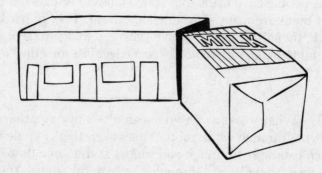

HOUSES   Almost any empty container can become a building of some kind. We particularly like the waxed cardboard cartons that milk often comes in. They're easy to handle and surprisingly durable. The half-gallon and quart sizes make good skyscrapers.

Lying on its side, the quart size can also be a house trailer . . . or a row of store fronts. The pints and half pints are fine houses.

Some children may decide the containers are okay as houses just as they are. Others might want to try some decorating. Poster paints will cover most ordinary cardboard surfaces, but you'll probably need to glue construction paper to any surfaces—such as the milk cartons—that have waxy outsides. Then you can draw doors and windows and signs or anything you like. Some parents have even enjoyed cutting out the doors and windows.

Some buildings you make may need extra stability. If you carefully pull apart the pinched top of a milk carton and cut along the corners, you'll find you have four flaps that you can bend outwards. By turning the carton upside down, you can use them as a base for the building. You can tape these flaps down, but you could also do some "landscaping" by going rock hunting and piling the ones you collect on top of the flaps like paperweights.

Securing three of the four flaps will probably be enough. You can cut off the fourth entirely and make that side the front of the building. Or, if you cut that fourth flap a little higher into the side of the building, you can fold it into a simple sort of awning which a little car can drive under.

NIGHT-LIGHT   When Becky Galliucci was about four, she had lots of trouble going to bed because she was sure that every time her mother turned off the bedroom light, the closet door was going to swing open and let something scary out. Rena helped solve that problem by putting a night-light in her daughter's room—a small bulb that plugged directly into a wall socket along the floor.

But she did something else, too. She and Becky made a milk-carton building together—one with a cutout door and windows which could safely fit over the night-light. That building became the start of a little village in Becky's bedroom, and at bedtime she and her parents would make up stories about what might be going on there.

Here's how they did it.

They took an empty half-gallon milk carton and started by cutting off the part that had been opened—just the triangular shape around what had been the spout. Next, they cut down the middle of the same side from top to bottom . . . and along the bottom of either side of that cut. Once they'd done that, the back of the building consisted of two flaps that could be opened up and bent outwards.

They then cut out the square bottom piece altogether, and they also cut along the two side "shoulders" of the carton so that the whole thing could lie flat.

They made sure that what had been the inside of the carton was really dry, spread an all-purpose glue all over it *except* for the side flaps, and then applied a sheet of aluminum foil to the part they had glued. The aluminum foil was really a safety precaution so that the milk-carton house wouldn't get hot from the light, but as it turned out, the foil also gave the interior a wonderful shimmer.

With the house still laid flat, Becky drew windows and a door

on the foil. Her mother used a pair of sharp nail scissors to cut out the shapes Becky had drawn, cutting into the foil side because that way it was easier to keep the foil smooth and flat. (Rena said that, all the same, the foil got a bit wrinkled and torn as she was doing the cutting, but that it didn't matter at all.)

When the glue had dried, they taped the carton's side shoulders back in place again, and the building was finished. It fitted right over the night-light with space to spare and plenty of openings for air to circulate and heat to escape. Finally they kept the two side flaps bent outwards and taped them to the wall so that the building couldn't move about or fall over.

When we're making things with our children, we may want them to turn out fancier than they have to be. After all, our imaginations are in some ways greater than our children's, as are our abilities to work with our hands. I've often seen grown-ups give in to the temptation to alter what a child is doing in play—to make it more "correct," or realistic, or in some way more satisfying to grown-up expectations. It's not easy to resist such a temptation, as I found in my own work with children.

In encouraging our children's play, though, I believe our role is to offer support, cooperation . . . and help *when we're asked for it.* When we show our appreciation for what our children are trying to do in their own ways and within their own capabilities, we are helping them feel that their efforts are worthwhile and that they can take pride in their accomplishments.

Of course, we need to have those feelings about what we do, too. If we have the urge to make as fancy a building as we can out of a milk carton, then we ought to go ahead and do it! That's what play is for. All that matters is that the project becomes *our* project rather than our notion of what our children ought to be doing. We may even find that we need our children's help in carrying out what we're trying to do—just as they sometimes need ours. That kind of cooperative play can bring really good feelings to grown-ups and children alike, and a special building—post office, police station, fire house, or whatever—that Dad or Mom made may take on a lot of importance in the "village."

PEOPLE It's hard to make people, particularly if we're too ambitious about what they should look like or what they should be able to do. Making a toy person that can both stand and sit, for instance, is quite a challenge! In fact, few of the miniature figures available commercially can do both.

You've probably noticed that your children's early drawings of people aren't very realistic at all. Their drawings may be all head or mostly body, or a head with legs, or a body without arms. They represent people without looking much like people, but they're enough to satisfy a child's feelings about people at that time. It's much the same with the toy people children may play

with. They don't have to be more than representations for children to find them satisfying.

Spools of thread are simple and sturdy and colorful, and they come in different sizes that may suggest different family members. All you need is a pipe-cleaner head with a neck you can stick into the hole in the spool. (Incidentally, small spool people will fit nicely into egg-carton vehicles.) In addition to the sizes of the spools, their colors—and the colors you choose for the heads—may suggest who's who in the family.

Martha Warninski's daughter, Margot, is off at college in the Southwest right now studying engineering. According to Martha, she liked playing with spool people when she was little. We wrote her a note asking her to tell us about what she remembered. She sent us a long letter back, and in it she told us that she's babysitting in her spare time and *still* plays with spool people, only now they've become fancier. Here's what she does with them now:

"The kids and I start with normal size spools—about 1¾" long—and a bunch of different colored 8" pipe cleaners. We really didn't know at first what we were going to do and just made it up as we went along.

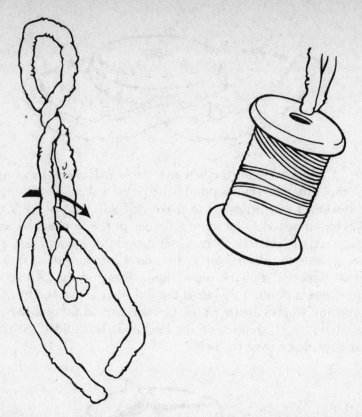

"First, we twisted a loop into the middle of a pipe cleaner to make a head, wrapping the two ends around each other to make one strand for the neck. Then we twisted the end of that strand around the middle of another pipe cleaner, bending it in half so that there would be two long skinny legs below the spool when we threaded the pipe cleaners through the hole.

"Next, we experimented with arms. What we finally did was to twist the ends of two pipe cleaners together so that we had one long one. We wrapped it around the top of the spool just under the rim. We placed the spool in the center, bent the pipe cleaners around to the back where we twisted them twice to keep them tight. Then we brought the 'arms' back around to the front where we had begun.

"When we made the first one, the kids decided it was going to be the Momma. They wanted her to have a skirt. Something else I did when I was little was to make doll skirts out of baking cups. There happened to be some foil ones in the kitchen, so we used those. All I did was to turn one upside down and cut a criss-cross—side to side and top to bottom. I lifted up these four triangular flaps and slid the pipe-cleaner legs and the bottom of the spool down inside. I squeezed the foil tight above the spool's bottom rim, wound another pipe cleaner around the foil like a belt, twisted it tight, snipped off the long ends, and folded the triangular flaps down over the belt.

"I don't know whose idea it was to slide plastic drinking straws over the pipe-cleaner legs and arms. I think one of the kids was just fiddling around and did it more or less by accident . . . but then we decided we liked the idea, so that was what we did. We cut the straws so that there was about an inch or so of pipe cleaner sticking out, and this we bent and twisted into little loops that made hands and feet. The hands could actually hold something if you wanted them to.

"As it turned out, the straws were a really good idea. They gave the pipe-cleaner limbs some extra stability, and they also bent and held their shape when you wanted to put the arms and legs into a particular position.

"Well, anyway, we did all the same things to make the Poppa spool person. The kids wanted him to have pants, and that really made us scratch our heads for a while! We tried all sorts of things without any luck at all, until I started playing with a couple of penny rolls I found in a desk drawer. You know, they're the heavy brown paper sleeves you get at the bank to hold fifty pennies together.

"We folded two of these in half lengthways—one for each leg. (Poppa's legs also had straws on them for strength.) We'd cut the pants short enough so that there was pipe cleaner sticking out to make feet. After trying for a while, we found it worked best to put the pants on so the fold in the pant leg was on the inside of the leg . . . with the leg running through the bottom channel in the folded paper. (If you see what I mean?!)

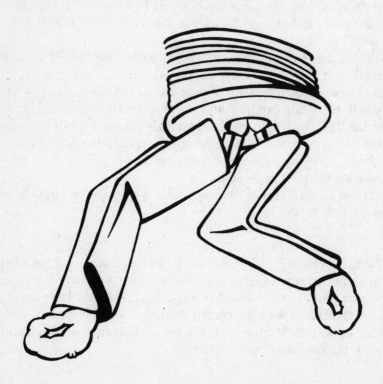

"Finally, I cut out two snapshots—one of the kids' mother and one of their father—and glued them on the pipe-cleaner heads. What delighted the kids the most was that because of the skirt and the sizes of the snapshots, the momma looked a little bigger than the poppa. In real life, she's about 5'4" and he's about 6'2". The kids thought it was a howl!

"We still haven't found a way to make these spool people stand. They can only sit. I guess that's going to have to be my next *serious* engineering project!"

We asked Margot how the children had played with spool Momma and spool Poppa, and she told us that most often they just get brought into whatever play the children are doing at the time. They've been out to the sandbox, and they've been propped up on a "park bench" (*see page 202*) under a bush while the children played nearby.

The other day Margot passed the four-year-old in the living room just when he was scolding spool Momma. It wasn't clear what Momma had done, but the boy was looking very stern, shaking his finger, and saying: "Now you stay right there where I can see you!"

There are, naturally, lots of ways to make "people." They can be made out of bakers' clay, papier-mâché, cardboard or styrofoam. They can be made out of pine cones—with acorns or chestnuts as heads. They can be made out of spoons with painted faces, their handles stuck into modeling-dough stands. Or out of little plastic or heavy glass bottles—the kind some children's medicines, eye drops, glue or typewriter correction fluid come in—with pipe cleaner heads stuck in the tops.

It isn't what's fancy that appeals; it's whatever appeals to your family's fancy.

TREES & THINGS On the underside of many bushes and hedges you can find leafless twigs that look like wintertime trees in miniature. They may be less than a foot long, but they have a stem and, at the end, a well developed system of little branches. Collecting these tiny winter trees could be the purpose of a stroll through the neighborhood or park.

Once you have a supply on hand, you can give them foliage with cotton balls, either stuffing the balls in among the branchlike twigs, or pulling the balls apart gently to make veils you can drape over, around and about the branches. If you feel the trees need to be green, a light coating of spray paint will do it; or a light, fine spray of vegetable coloring applied with the kind of sprayer you may use for dampening clothes when ironing.

You can make trees out of paper, too. One simple way is to take a white or colored sheet of 8½″ × 11″ paper and cut it in half lengthwise. Then roll one of the halves into a little cylinder about as wide inside as your little finger. You'll want to tape it so that it stays together, and the band of tape should go about ½″ or so from the end you decide will be the bottom of the tree.

At the end that will be the top of the tree, you need to cut about five slits that go roughly halfway down the cylinder . . . and then, by pushing and turning gently with your little finger inside the bottom of the cylinder, you'll see the tree begin to sprout. Once you've got it started, you may find it easier to pull the tree up from the top. You'll find the "branches" will come out in a

corkscrew pattern, and you can bend them down any way you think looks good. You can cut them more if you like, or trim and shape them, too.

Now, if you make four cuts at the bottom of the tree (on opposite sides of the cylinder and running just up to the bottom of the tape), you'll have four tabs you can bend outward and tape to the floor or table to keep the tree upright. You could also make a bakers' clay stand if you prefer: a flat base with a small column in the center which the trunk of the tree can fit over.

Cotton balls all by themselves make good shrubs, and so do bunches of cotton-swab ends—particularly if you tug gently on the cotton to stretch it out and then spread it into clumps. Both trees and shrubs will probably need modeling-clay bases.

Green felt or green construction paper can become patches of pretend lawn, and if you want to go on with the landscaping project by adding flowers, one suggestion is to cut very small pieces off those kitchen sponges that come in several colors. You can use dabs of glue to stick them under trees, around houses and lawns, or wherever you think a little color would look good.

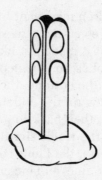

TRAFFIC LIGHTS & STOP SIGNS For very young children, recognizing red and green—and what they mean—can be enough of a game. Four tongue depressors, glued together at the edges to form a hollow square, will make a four-sided column that can stand by itself or be stuck in a bakers'-clay base to make it steadier. On each panel you can draw two circles, one beneath the other, and then color the top ones on two opposite sides red and the bottom ones on the other sides green.

Placed on a corner at a crossroads, or in the middle of an intersection if the road is wide enough, this traffic light can let you play stop-and-go games with one or more cars coming from different directions. Don't be surprised if children of even three or four don't seem to be able to "obey the rules" yet; at that age, the understanding of what rules and limits are may still be forming. When you're out in a car together, you'll have a chance to talk more about traffic lights, what they mean, and why people are careful to observe the safety limits that traffic lights set.

Older children may want to include the yellow light on their traffic signal. We've seen a six-sided version that had three lights on each panel. It is made just like the four-sided one we described above, but out of six tongue depressors instead. If the light facing you is green (on the bottom), then the one on the next panel to the left will be yellow (in the middle), and the next to the left will be red (at the top), then back to green . . . and to yellow . . . and to red. So long as the traffic signal is always turned to the right (or counter-clockwise), the lights come up in the right sequence.

If you want an even fancier traffic light, you can go one step further. Instead of making colored circles on the panels, you can glue on bottle caps where the circles would go. Inside the cap that is supposed to be lit, you then stick a circle of the proper-colored paper.

Stop signs have eight sides. If you trace a circle on a piece of cardboard, flatten the top and bottom with short lines, flatten the sides with short lines, and join the ends of the short lines with diag-

ᴄnals, you'll have approximately the right shape. Once you've made one that looks okay to you, you can cut it out and use it for tracing others—and for tracing the same shapes out of red construction paper to cover them. If the construction paper seems heavy enough, you may not need the cardboard at all.

After painting or crayoning on a white STOP, the signs can be glued onto popsicle sticks and stuck into clay bases at the intersections where you decide they belong.

FIRE HYDRANTS   How about painting some corks red and gluing them down here and there? Your children could suggest where the hydrants could be placed. (Have they seen some in your neighborhood?)

MAIL BOXES   The large-size kitchen match boxes aren't as easy to find as they used to be, but they're still around. Empty, of course, and decorated if you want them to be, they have always made popular places for children to keep special treasures. Standing on end, the boxes can also make mail drops. By leaving the drawer open a half inch or so at the top, you can drop "letters" in.

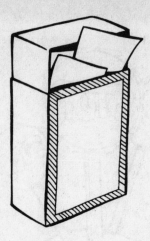

When the mail carrier comes by for a pickup, you can push the drawer down and shut, slide the sleeve up a little, and collect the letters at the bottom.

To whom were the letters addressed? Can they be delivered?

BENCHES   Two pairs of popsicle sticks, one stick glued crosswise over the other to make an X, can serve as the framework for a bench. A tongue depressor laid flat between the Xs (like a log in a sawbuck) can make the seat. You'll need to glue it in place to keep it steady, and you may want to add another tongue depressor, laid along the first one and against the arms of the Xs, to make a back for the bench.

If, when you're done, you think the bench is too high off the ground, just snip off the legs of the Xs to the height you want.

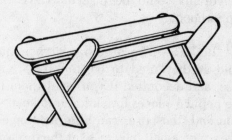

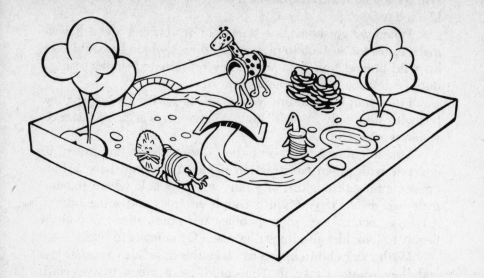

Making a Zoo

More and more zoos nowadays have open-air habitats where the animals can roam around with some sense of freedom and space. These sorts of habitats are certainly kinder ways to keep animals in captivity than are cages, and for most of us, it's more fun to watch animals roaming about than just pacing back and forth behind bars. Some very young children, though, can find these large open enclosures scary, and Stefano Galliucci was one such child.

I remember going to an open-air zoo with the Galliuccis when Stefano was four. At that zoo, you could ride in a sort of chairlift over some of the places where the wild animals were kept. There they were, right below you, looking as free as you please. Stefano was terrified and cried and clung to his father all during the ride.

I mentioned to Victor that I'd learned that many young children who were trying to master their own urges to bite found wild animals frightening: wild animals represented a lot of unrestrained biting power!

Victor smiled. "Stefano *is* having a problem with that," he said. "Just a week ago he got mad at Victor Jr. and bit him on the arm. When he realized what he'd done, he was terribly upset, just like today."

When we got home, we started brainstorming about how to make cages for Stefano to play with—places where he could keep his wild animal toys (and what they represented) under control until he felt ready to let them roam free.

For a simple enclosure, you could start with a large, shallow box with sides only 2" or 3" high. A large pizza box, for instance, would work well.

You might want to paint the bottom of the box green, or cover it with green construction paper. You could have a blue creek running through it, or a blue watering hole where the animals can drink. If you add a couple of trees and some bushes, maybe a rock or two, some pebbles and pine cones . . . Well, it begins to look like an interesting place for animals to live.

With older children, you can take this basic idea as far as you and they want to take it. You could use a green plastic cloth draped over some humps of crumpled-up newspaper, or make papier-mâché hills on top of the cloth. You might even make channels out of bakers' clay—or a pool—that could hold real water.

If you have a yard and the right kind of weather, the whole habitat can take shape out on the grass, and that could be the best place of all.

CAGES Shoeboxes make good cages, but any long and narrow box with a removable top will do.

One of the ends of the box can be the door of the cage. You can cut it along the bottom and along one side so that it is attached to the box only by its other side. Once you've bent it back and forth a couple of times, it will seem to swing on a hinge.

You can cut a panel out of the middle of this door, leaving an inch or so around the edges. And you can cut out long windows of the same height in the sides of the box. We suggest that these side windows *not* go the full length of the box—maybe about two-thirds of the distance from the door to the back—but it doesn't really matter. The reason for the suggestion, though, is that you might like to cut the top of the box to fit on just the last third of the cage so that the animal can have at least a little shelter and privacy.

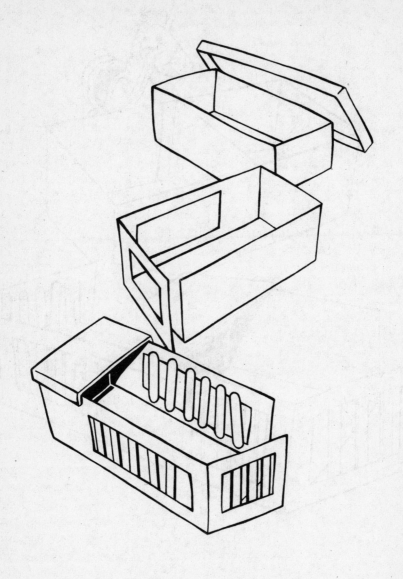

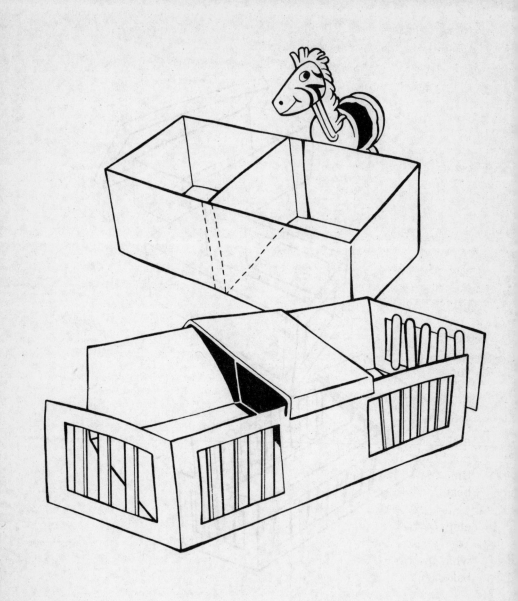

Cages have bars, of course, and you can make these with narrow strips of cardboard cut from the part of the top you don't use for the sheltering roof. If you'd rather, you can glue popsicle sticks up and down across the openings.

If you decide to have more than one cage, you might want to make another cage a double one. In this case, both ends become doors of the kind we described above. There needs to be a central partition, and this can be made out of part of the top, or out of another piece of cardboard. If you cut the partition about an inch or so wider than the box, you'll be able to make two narrow flaps you can fold and glue to the sides of the box. (It seems to work best if you fold the two flaps in opposite directions, and you'll have to keep gentle pressure on the sides while the glue dries.)

With this double cage, you might consider making the side windows run about halfway from the doors to the partition. (There will be two windows on each side now.) That way, you can cut out a piece of the top to fit over the part of the box that doesn't have openings in it. There will still be a place on either side of the partition where the animals can find a roof over their heads.

We can imagine three of these kinds of cages set up around a shallow bowl of water that has rocks all around it . . . and a flat rock in the middle of the water that looks like an island. What do your children suppose might be living *there*?

ANIMALS   It takes more talent than most of us may have to make homemade animals that really look like what they're supposed to be. Fortunately, all that matters here is having a good time together playing with whatever is at hand, regardless of the beauty or accuracy of our creations.

Some animals, particularly the heavy, chunky ones such as elephants, rhinos and hippos, lend themselves to clay modeling. You might want to experiment with soft modeling clay first to see what you can come up with, and then duplicate a shape you like in bakers' clay that will harden and can then be painted.

To make a more delicate animal—a giraffe, say—you could start with three inches of cardboard tubing of the size that comes in paper towel or toilet tissue. At the very front and very back of

the tube you can wrap pipe cleaners, twisting them together a couple of times and then spreading them to make spindly legs. Depending on how long your pipe cleaners are to begin with, you may have to join two together. And depending on how long you want the legs to be, you may have to wrap them around the tube more than once. Putting plastic straws over the pipe-cleaner legs will make them stronger.

A tongue depressor can make a giraffelike neck. You'll have to cut a slit just behind the pipe cleaner that's making up the front legs and slide the depressor into the tube on an angle so that the neck is pointing forward somewhat. You can wipe a little glue on the end inside the tube so that it will stick to the bottom where it touches. A little more glue along the top edge of the slit on either side of the depressor may help keep the neck steady, too.

You'll need a head, but a very simple shape will do. If you cut two identical shapes out of cardboard, you can glue one on each side at the top of the tongue-depressor neck, sticking the one to the other at the "nose" end of the head.

Do you think you need a tail? If so, you could stick on 3″ or so of yarn, unravelling the end, perhaps, to make a tassel.

A funny-looking giraffe, that's for sure! You could paint or color all the parts if you wanted to. How would it look if you stuffed a shredded cotton ball or two into the front opening of the cardboard tube—the place where the giraffe's chest would be?

Here's another Galliucci recipe—this one for a thread-spool lion. We made one and it had a lot of character. You might like to try making one, too.

First, you push five pipe cleaners through the hole in a large thread spool. They might all be the same color, except for one red one. The pipe cleaners should stick out one end about 1″ or so, with the rest sticking out the other end. You can make the tail by twisting the long ends together, but you might leave them spread out into a tassel at the very tip.

Then you can take a small cupcake paper and draw anything you think looks like a lion's ears, eyes, and nose in the circle at the bottom. The bottom of the nose you've drawn should fall right about in the center of the circle. The ridged sides, flattened out a little, become the lion's mane.

Now you want to poke a hole just below the lion's nose and push all five pipe cleaners through it so that the bottom of the cupcake paper pushes up tight against the flat end of the spool. It will stay there when you spread four of the pipe cleaners apart, two in each direction to make whiskers. And the fifth one, the red one, can be bent into a loop with the end tucked back in the hole in the spool . . . to make a tongue.

Two more pipe cleaners make the legs, wrapped around the spool next to the front and back rims, twisted underneath to keep them tight, and then spread and bent to make legs and paws. Right behind the front legs you might want to wrap several more pipe cleaners (each twisted onto the next to make one long strand), so that the lion will have a softer body and the look of having shoulders. When you get to the end of the strand, just tuck the end under any of the wrappings that have gone before and push the sharp tip of the last pipe cleaner well into the rest with your fingernail. (In fact, you might want to check carefully for any other sharp tips that may be sticking out here and there and push them down, too, so that they can't accidentally prick a finger.)

Another way to make animals is to cut out any pictures of them you can find in magazines and mount them on cardboard that you've cut to the same shape as the pictures. If you stick a paper clip in a bakers' clay base when the clay is wet and squeeze the clay tight around the clip, you'll have a little stand for your animal cutouts.

Things to Make and Eat

There's a lot to learn about how the world works when it comes to the preparing of food. How does food grow? Who picks it and how? How does it get packaged and get to the store? There are many people who help get food from its natural state to the table, and you might want to talk with your child about some familiar kinds of food and how they get to you to eat. Unless young children ask, I wouldn't get into explaining the details of meat and poultry production. Young children often identify strongly with helpless creatures.

Once food gets to your house and the preparing and cooking begins, there's a whole lot more to think about—things like hot and cold, full and empty, measurements of all kinds, and there's stirring, mixing, folding and kneading, baking, frying and boiling, and lots of examples of how things can change yet still be the same. For instance, water can become ice or steam, eggs can take many shapes, and things like rice and butter can change from hard to soft.

We're often asked for some of the recipes that we've used on *Mister Rogers' Neighborhood,* and so we thought we'd include a few of them here—as well as some of our other favorites.

Tofu with Onions and Cheese Sauce

1 box frozen prepared Welsh rarebit
2 medium-size onions, thinly sliced
4–6 tbs. oil
10 oz. firm tofu, cut into ½″ slices
Garlic salt

Defrost and melt Welsh rarebit in double boiler. Salt each side of tofu slices with garlic salt. Flour each tofu slice and fry in butter until crisp and brown. Cook onions in oil until tender. Place onions on top of tofu and top with the Welsh rarebit.

Banana Boat

1 slice white bread
Peanut butter
1 banana
2 thin pretzel sticks

Spread peanut butter on a slice of white bread. Slice a banana in half lengthwise and place the halves on the bread. Fold the bread in half to make a "boat." Insert two thin pretzel sticks into the sides, like oars, to hold the bread together.

Quick and Easy Fish Fillets

2 lbs. fish fillets
4 tbs. melted butter or margarine
¾ cup dry white wine
1 tsp. parsley flakes
½ tsp. garlic powder
½ tsp. dried green onion flakes
Paprika
½ cup toasted slivered almonds
Lemon slices

Lay fillets in baking dish. Mix melted butter and wine and pour over fish. Sprinkle with parsley, onions, garlic powder, and paprika. Put in 400° oven for 20 minutes. Take out and sprinkle with toasted almonds. Serve with lemon slices (and tartar sauce, if you like).

Chef Brockett's Nutritious Snack

¾ cup nonfat dry milk
1 cup peanut butter
1 tbs. margarine
½ cup chopped nuts
½ cup raisins
½ cup dates (optional)
Graham cracker crumbs (optional)

Soften margarine and mix with peanut butter. Add dry milk and mix thoroughly. Add raisins, nuts, and dates and shape into balls. Roll in Graham cracker crumbs.

José's Arroz Con Leche (Rice with Milk)

1 cup rice
Cinnamon sticks
Peel of one orange
1 large can evaporated milk
½ can condensed milk
Vanilla
Raisins
Powdered cinnamon

Boil rice with cinnamon sticks and orange peel. Drain. Add evaporated milk, condensed milk, a dash of vanilla flavoring. Cook on stovetop to pudding like consistency. Stir in raisins. Serve in small cups and sprinkle with powdered cinnamon.

(If you prefer, you could use toasted coconut, apples, or apricots instead of raisins, and nutmeg instead of cinnamon, and add banana slices as a topping.)

Granola

½ cup honey
1 cup vegetable oil
3 cups rolled oats
1 cup dried milk
1 cup shredded coconut
2 cups untoasted wheat germ (if toasted, add later)

1 cup sesame seeds
1 cup sunflower seeds
1 cup crushed raw peanuts
Raisins or other dried fruit

Mix honey and vegetable oil and spread on the bottom of a large pan. Distribute oats, dried milk, coconut, wheat germ on the bottom of the pan. Bake at 350° for 40 minutes, stirring every 5 minutes until well toasted. Mix sesame seeds, sunflower seeds, and peanuts together and add to oven-toasted mixture when it has cooled. Add raisins or any other dried fruit you like.

Platanos Fritos (Fried Bananas)

Bananas, several
Cinnamon
Brown sugar
Juice of 1 lemon
Butter

Cut the bananas lengthwise and sprinkle with cinnamon, brown sugar and lemon juice. Fry in uncovered pan until they are tender.

Noodle Pudding

½ lb. cooked noodles (wide)
½ pint sour cream
½ lb. creamed cottage cheese
½ tsp. salt
½ cup sugar
¼ lb. melted butter or margarine
1 small can cling peaches (sliced and drained)

Combine all ingredients and bake uncovered at 350° for 1 hour.

Soft Pretzels

This recipe comes from Judy Liskin-Gasparro and Christopher Gasparro in Lawrenceville, New Jersey.

1 package yeast
1 tbs. sugar
1½ cups warm water
4 cups unbleached white flour
1 egg, beaten
Coarse salt (such as kosher salt)

Combine yeast, warm water and sugar in a large bowl. (The

water should feel slightly warmer than skin temperature.) Stir to dissolve yeast. Add flour, stirring well after the addition of each cupful. (By the addition of the last cupful, the batter may be too stiff to stir.) Turn out the batter onto a floured board and knead until the dough is smooth and the flour is incorporated. Break off small lumps of dough and shape any way you want. Put the shapes on an ungreased cookie sheet. Brush on beaten egg with pastry brush, then sprinkle with coarse salt. Bake in preheated oven at 425° until golden brown. The actual time will depend on the thickness of the shapes you have made. When done, the shapes should be put on a rack to cool.

Tip: When you're baking with children, encourage them not to lick the dough off their fingers. If they do, everything will begin to get sticky. Dry, floured hands are best for kneading.

Tofu Burgers

20 oz. firm tofu
1 cup chopped onions
3 tablespoons oil
⅔ cup bread crumbs
2 tbs. Worcestershire sauce
1 tbs. soy sauce
Garlic salt, to taste
3 eggs, beaten

Cook chopped onions in oil until tender but not brown. Cool. Drain tofu and crumble with fingertips. Add all ingredients to crumbled tofu and mix well. Make into burgers. Fry in butter until crisp and evenly browned on both sides.

Vegetable Burgers

1½ cups dry lentils
1 medium onion
2 cloves garlic
¼ lb. fresh mushrooms
1 stalk celery
2 small carrots
1 small green pepper
1 cup walnuts
1 tsp. salt
1 tsp. chili powder
½ tsp. dry mustard

½ tsp. ground cumin
freshly ground black pepper
2 beaten eggs
5 tbs. tomato paste
¼ cup rolled oats, bread crumbs or wheat germ
Worcestershire sauce

Place lentils in a medium pot with 4–5 cups water. Don't add salt. Bring to boil, then simmer for 30 minutes (if you've soaked the lentils in cold water for a couple of hours beforehand) or 45 minutes (if you've started with dry lentils). The lentils should be tender throughout, but not mushy. When they're done, drain them.

Dice finely the onion, garlic, mushrooms, celery, green pepper and walnuts, Sauté together in butter.

Add to the sauté the salt, chili powder, dry mustard, cumin and black pepper. When the vegetables and nuts are well seasoned and tender, remove the sauté from heat and add to the cooked lentils. Mix together in a large bowl.

Add beaten eggs, tomato paste, rolled oats (or alternatives), and Worcestershire sauce to taste.

Mix everything together until well combined. The mixture should be fairly solid. Shape into burgers about ¼" thick and as large as you like. If there is time, chill for one hour before cooking.

To cook, either fry on both sides in butter, or broil, turning once, until brown. Serve on whole grain rolls with sprouts, tomatoes and all your favorite burger toppings. Cheddar cheese melted or broiled on top is nice, too.

Leftover burgers may be wrapped and frozen (cooked or uncooked) to be used at a later time.

Spaghetti Marco Polo

When Julia Child came to visit us on *Mister Rogers' Neighborhood*, this is the dish she showed us how to make. We asked her to write down the recipe for it, and here it is.

"Spaghetti Marco Polo is easy to make, full of vim, vigor and good things, and a wonderful change from the old tomato sauce jazz. Half a pound of spaghetti will give 4 good servings, and you don't need much more than a salad to make a whole main course of it.

"½ lb. spaghetti (look on the package to make sure it says 'made from #1 semolina')

A large pan of boiling salted water

A large serving bowl or platter, and long-handled serving fork and spoon

⅔ cup chopped walnuts or peanuts (more or less)

About ½ cup chopped black olives (these come already chopped in a can)

About ½ cup chopped red pimiento (sweet red pepper, peeled, seeded, and packed in a jar. Be sure they are *not* packed in vinegar)

About ⅓ cup chopped fresh parsley

1 tbs. or so chopped fresh chives

Salt and pepper to taste

About ¾ cup grated Swiss or Parmesan cheese (this should be fresh to have the best taste)

About 4 tbs. olive oil

"About 10 minutes before you are to have dinner, put the spaghetti on to boil, following the directions on the package. While it's boiling, mix the nuts, olives, pimiento and herbs in a bowl with a little sprinkling of salt and pepper (not too much). Be sure to taste the spaghetti frequently so that it doesn't get overcooked. It should have the slightest crunch at the very inside when you chew it. It should not get soft and mushy. When it's done, immediately drain it by pouring it into a big colander, and you may need some help with this. Shake the colander to get rid of all water dribbles.

"Pour the olive oil into the serving platter or bowl, and toss the spaghetti about in the oil until every strand looks covered. Then toss it quickly with salt and pepper, and taste to be sure it is just right. Scoop the nut and herb mixture on top, and bring the spaghetti to the table, along with the cheese.

"At the table, toss the herbs and nuts into the spaghetti, sprinkling bits of cheese into it as you go. Use big dramatic lifting movements, raising the spaghetti high, and clacking the fork and spoon together. Do this rather rapidly, as though you were a maître d'hôtel in a great restaurant (but don't let the spaghetti get cold!). When you feel you have tossed enough, scoop up serving portions, lifting high again, and place them on each plate.

"You can eat the spaghetti with a fork and knife, but have you ever tried chopsticks?

"Bon appetit!"

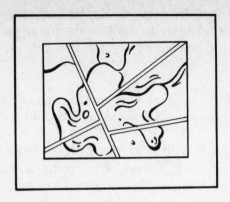

Some Other Ideas

STAINED GLASS   Here's a way to play with color, heat and light—and to make a permanent display for a kitchen or bedroom window.

You'll need crayon shavings, but you don't need a very sharp knife to get the kind of slivers you want—a butter knife, plastic picnic knife or a potato peeler will generally do. If you're not using something sharp, your child might enjoy helping with the shaving.

You're going to distribute the shavings on a piece of wax paper, and you may want to make piles of different-colored shavings before you do so, or you can let the shavings fall directly onto the paper in a random fashion.

The next step is to cover the first piece of wax paper with another the same size, so that you have a crayon-shaving sandwich. Now, press the two together with a warm iron, making the shavings melt and run into flowing designs. Once your creation has cooled, the two sheets of paper should be well stuck together.

To make a frame for your piece of "stained glass," you can cut a window in a piece of construction paper—a window that's just a little smaller than the size of the wax-paper sheets. Mat board makes an even better frame because it's sturdier, but of course it's a little more difficult to cut. If you have the inclination and the patience, you can even make a fancy window that has cutout designs in it rather than just one big opening.

However you decide to do it, the final step is to tape your piece of stained glass to the back of the frame you've made, and then put it in a place where daylight can shine through it.

COIN BANKS   Saving coins, even just pennies, is a good way to learn more about counting, about money, and about buying and selling.

Any container with a lid (in which to cut a slit) and a wide mouth can be a bank. Yogurt, sour cream, and margarine tubs work well, as do jelly jars and the like. Glass containers have the advantage of letting a child see how full they're getting. And once they *are* full, you and your child can set off to the store together to trade the contents for a small toy, some crayons, or a healthy snack.

(As with anything small, you'll need to be watchful that the pennies get put in the bank and not in the mouth.)

PARACHUTES   Anything that flies or floats in the air seems to have a powerful fascination for children—a fascination many of us can still feel whether we're looking at a helium balloon or a 747. How do these things stay up? Why don't they fall like we do?

The fascinations and dreams of childhood are often the raw materials of creativity and invention. Everything man-made was first an idea, and those ideas that people pursued and turned into realities were often those that touched them most deeply.

These parachutes won't stay up long, but all the same you may find your child wanting to see them doing their seemingly magical floating descents over and over again.

You'll need a square of thin material about the size of a large handkerchief, along with four lengths of light string for each parachute you make. Eight-inch lengths should be about right. One end of the pieces of string gets tied to each corner of the cloth. Here are two ideas for what to do with the other ends.

(1) Tie them to a metal nut or washer, making sure the lengths of string remain about equal once you've tied the knots. Now you can fold up the cloth, wrap the strings around it, and throw the whole package up in the air as high as you can. (If you

have a tennis racquet, you might be able to knock it up a good deal higher than you can throw it.) You may need to experiment with the weight at the ends of the strings, too, if your parachute isn't floating well.

(2) Poke four evenly spaced holes around the rim of a paper cup and tie the strings to the cup. You might find the easiest way is to thread the strings through the holes (from the inside or outside, it doesn't matter) and then tie a knot in the ends that's too big to pass back through the holes. You'll have to put something in the cup to give it weight: toy people . . . toy animals . . . a block . . . pebbles . . . a cookie? And you'll have to find a *safe* place to drop it from. If you choose a window, *you'd* best be the one to do the dropping, and you could send surprises down to your child on the ground below.

ACTIVITIES: AROUND THE NEIGHBORHOOD   219

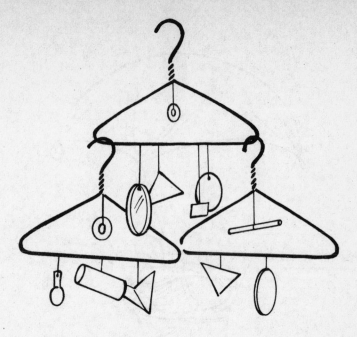

MOBILE   One simple way to make a mobile is to tie small objects on strings to the bottom bar of a wire coat hanger. You could use metal washers, pieces of wood, construction-paper shapes, silver foil, small measuring spoons, plastic container lids . . . just about anything. The effect will be more interesting if each object hangs at a different level, and you'll have to experiment with which objects go where on the bar so that the hanger balances evenly.

Once you've decided on your arrangement, you can tie one end of a piece of string to the hanger's hook, and the other end to a small nail placed wherever you want the mobile to hang. You might want to choose a place where there's a breeze to make the objects spin and sway.

You can make your mobile more complicated if you want to by hanging two more coat hangers from the first one—one from each bottom corner. You'll need to secure them in position with tight loops of thread so they don't slide back and forth. You can take this project still further by adding four more hangers—two on each of the ones you just tied on to the first. Now, when you begin attaching objects to this tree-shaped frame, you'll have to be *very* careful about weight and balance. You don't have to restrict yourself to hanging things from the bars, either; you can also tie them to the necks of the hangers so that they spin around in the middle of the hangers' frames.

You'll need plenty of space to let one of these big mobiles hang free. A porch might be a good place. You could even hang one from the branch of a tree.

(If your first hanger—the top one—is one of those that's covered in paper, it will act as a sail and make your mobile more active in light breezes. You'll still be able to hang things from it by poking holes through the paper along the bar.)

WEIGHTS & MEASURES   Part of understanding early childhood is remembering that there are many basic concepts about ourselves and our world that we now take for granted but that once were unfamiliar and even mysterious. There was a time, for instance, when *inside* and *outside* had no real meaning for us. The same was true for *full* and *empty, heavy* and *light.* As you watch very young children playing, you'll often be able to see them experimenting with these concepts. They haven't the words for them yet, but they're finding out what these concepts mean in practice.

Early play may be about a single concept, but later play is likely to be about how several concepts go together—for instance, about how when you put something *inside* something else so that the container gets *full,* the container also gets *heavy.*

A bag of dried beans (or unpopped popcorn) and a small plastic cup can start a young child on an exploration of these concepts, and you may be surprised how naturally these explorations seem to take place. Even at a year old, a child may be fascinated for minutes on end by putting the beans into the cup and taking them out again. Or by filling the cup and emptying it. If you add a second cup to this kind of play, sooner or later your child is likely to start pouring the beans from one cup into the other, back and forth. An older child may be intrigued by the question of whether a half-filled cup is really half full or half empty. A much older child might even be able to relate these questions to the concepts of *optimism* and *pessimism!*

There's really no end to where this kind of play can lead. If you added a flat ruler and a pencil to your cups and beans, you could set off on a whole new set of explorations about *balance* by building a little seesaw. If the cups are the same and the pencil is under the midpoint of the ruler, we know that a full cup will go down and an empty one will go up.

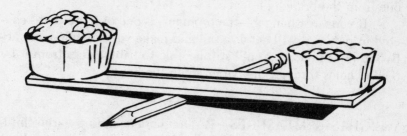

That may be quite a discovery for a young child!

Trying to make the cups balance is a lot more difficult, and a child will have to be several years old to understand that the same number of beans in each cup is likely to bring the seesaw into balance. But when a child does arrive at that understanding, he or she is already learning about mathematical "equations" without even knowing there are such things. What happens to the balanced seesaw when you take two beans away from each side? Or when you add two beans to each side?

This is the kind of play that so often underlies scientific discovery later in life. For example, try putting a pencil under the 7″ mark on the ruler. Bringing the seesaw into balance is a different kind of game now, isn't it? If we played this new game long enough, we'd begin to understand something about the ratio of inches to weights and quantities. Putting our discoveries into words and symbols might remain beyond us all of our lives, but we *could* gain an understanding of a principle that applies in many other instances.

And just like scientists, children sometimes make "discoveries" that turn out to be mirages. After playing on real seesaws for a while, Victor Galliucci, Jr., at four years old, noticed that bigger children always went down while he always went up. That was fine, but he'd also concluded along the way that bigger children were always older than he was. As a result, the scientific "discovery" that he announced to his mother one day was that *older* children went down and *younger* children went up.

"That," said Rena, "took a lot of sorting out!"

BOATS If you take a waxed milk carton, lay it on its side with the opened spout facing upwards, and then cut it in half lengthwise around the sides, you'll have a sturdy hull for a boat. The pointed end makes a natural prow, and the craft should have enough stability to carry light cargo. You can give it ballast by putting a wad of modeling clay at about the midpoint of the bottom. You can also stick a drinking-straw mast in the modeling clay and affix a sail made of stiff paper. (The easiest way to do so might be to cut two slits in the sail and thread the straw through them.)

Pint-size cartons might suggest tug boats, quart-size ones ocean liners, and half-gallons could become low-sided barges. When afloat in a bathtub or pool, they'll each act differently.

Here's something you might want to try. Make a small hole in the middle of the back of the carton (the stern of the boat), and cut a thin slit down to the hole from the top of the back wall. Blow up a balloon and, stretching the mouthpiece part, work it down the slit to the hole, keeping the opening pinched shut on the outside of the boat. When you're ready, let go. How big you made the hole

will determine how fast the boat goes and for how long. You can try several variations using different-size cartons, altering the size of the hole, and varying the weight you put in the boat and where you put it. By experimenting, you may end up with a craft that moves really well.

You can also make a simple paddlewheeler out of a quart milk carton.

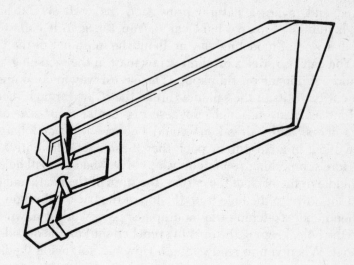

First, you open the top of the carton completely. If you look carefully at the open top, you'll see that two of the sides were pinched in and two weren't. What you want to do is to place the carton on its side, open end toward you, with one of the pinched-in parts on top.

Now, cut around the whole top about ½" *below* the top panel. This top piece is the hull of your boat. When you've turned it right way up, cut out the triangle at what was the open end so that you have a pointed "bow." Because this triangle was pinched in at the beginning, you'll probably find it bends upwards a little bit. That's good; the point will stay a little above the water.

Next, at the back of the boat, or the stern, cut an opening about 2" long and 1½" wide. Save the piece you cut out, trimming it at the front, back and sides so that it's smaller than the opening itself. This piece is the paddle of your paddlewheeler.

You'll need an elastic band—one that will stretch around the back of the boat where the opening is. Before you stretch it, though, poke two small holes in your paddle and thread the elastic through them. Then loop the ends of the elastic over the parts of the boat on either side of the opening.

You're ready now to wind up the paddle and see if it spins freely when you let go. Winding it one way will make the boat go forwards, the other way, backwards. Can you get your paddle-wheeler to go the full length of a bathtub?

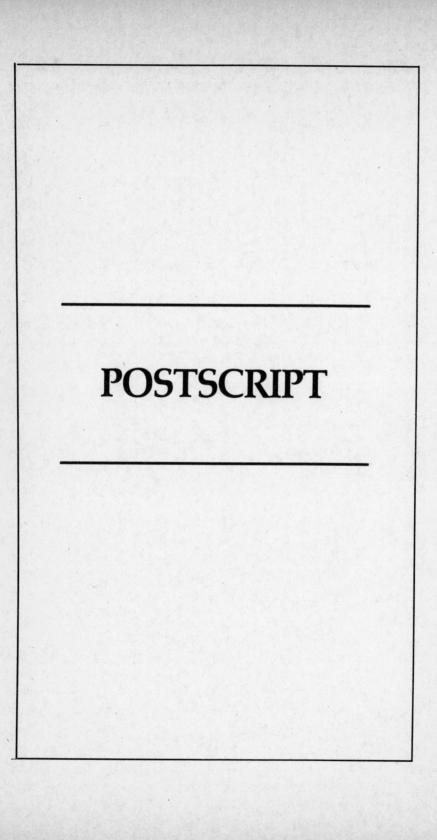

POSTSCRIPT

The chances are that you may read this postscript before you read most of the words that come before it. That's fine; this is a book to use any way you want to use it. If, in browsing through, your eye falls on a project you'd like to try, go ahead and try it—whether the project is at the beginning, middle or end. It certainly wasn't our intention to write a textbook!

We hope, though, that over time you will read the words that surround the suggested projects. There are plenty of books that provide lists of things to do when there isn't anything else to do. It wasn't our intention either just to add another title to that shelf in the library!

In fact, that's the very point. Play is so often talked about and written about as if it were a last resort and a relief from times of serious learning. In our book, however, play *is* serious learning, children's natural way.

Play is a natural way for adults to learn, too, all life long. The next time you find yourself wrestling with a problem that's difficult to resolve, you may be surprised at what happens if you turn it into purposeful play. You might try drawing a picture of the problem—in any way that comes to mind. You could try making up a story about the problem: a kind of fairy tale. Or you could take common everyday objects—corks, paper clips, whatever— and use them to represent parts of the problem. As you move them around, considering their relationships and how they do—or don't—go together, you may stumble on all kinds of new possibilities for associating them, or for forming them into new patterns, ways that wouldn't have occurred to you through normal, logical, "serious" thought.

And you're likely to *feel* differently about the problem after you've played about it for a while. A change in feeling can do a great deal to increase a person's openness to new solutions.

Play does seem to open up another part of the mind that is always there, but that, since childhood, may have become closed off and hard to reach. When we treat our children's play as seriously as it deserves, we are helping them feel the joy that's to be found in the creative spirit. We're helping ourselves stay in touch with that spirit, too.

Those *were* intentions of ours in writing this book, and we hope you'll find it a stimulating and playful companion. We're encouraged by one reaction to the manuscript. We showed it to the Galliuccis, and Victor Sr. sent us this reply:

> It's true that we played a lot with the children when they were growing up, but as, one by one, they've moved away, I realized from reading your proposed book that Rena and I are much less likely to engage in play than we used to be. We've gone and done what so many people do. We've stopped thinking of play as something appropriate for adults.
>
> But a funny thing happened. I came across your suggestion for a pendulum game—you know, the one where you try to knock over empty detergent bottles [*see page 136*]—and my mind took off in a similar but different direction. I took an empty detergent bottle, the kind with the nozzle that pulls out and pushes in to start and stop the flow, and turned it into a pendulum paintbrush. What I did was to cut out most of the bottom of the bottle, leaving only a narrow strip across the middle. Into that strip I screwed a very small eye screw.
>
> I bought a little swivel at the hardware store and attached it to a beam in the basement. I tied one end of a piece of string onto the swivel, and on the other end I tied a hook, the kind used

for hanging Christmas ornaments. The hook fit neatly and easily into the small eye screw in the bottom of the bottle.

Beneath this contraption, on the floor, I spread out a large piece of paper. To start with, I just put some black paint into the bottle, pulled out the nozzle, and set it swinging to see what would happen. What happened was that the paint splattered everywhere because I'd hung the bottle too high above the paper. Oh well, that was easy to fix. Come to think of it, some people might like it to splatter a little, but for my purposes, I found somewhere between 18" and 3' quite high enough! Whenever I wanted to stop painting, I caught the bottle and pushed in the nozzle.

Naturally, one thing led to another, and now I've got an array of detergent bottles I can interchange, each adding a new color and design to the same piece of paper.

The last work of pendulum art I did had a background of earth colors—browns, grays, russets, ochres and some deep purple. Then I did one swing with a sharp, fluorescent green. Wow!

It just so happens that we're trying to think up ideas for the cover of the next annual report for my laser-optics company. That pattern of green looked like a searing line of light, and I really think I hit on something. I'm not saying that my exact artwork will end up on the cover, but I'll bet we use something like it.

Thanks for sending me the manuscript. I'll send you the annual report.

Playfully yours,

Victor

P.S. Rena sends love.

And to you who read and use this book, we send the same wish we sent our children in the dedication: May you find ever-expanding playgrounds of the mind, body and spirit!

APPENDIX

MISTER ROGERS' NEIGHBORHOOD ACTIVITIES

Here is a list of activities you will find on *Mister Rogers' Neighborhood*. Many of them are similar to activities suggested in this book. To find out which programs you are currently watching, look for the program number at the very end of the broadcast.

We have reedited some of the older programs over the years, and in doing so have changed a few of the activities in the series. Every change may not be reflected in the following list, but we hope, nonetheless, that this index will be helpful to you.

Program #	Description of Activity
1005	Puppet-making
1013	Variety show
1017	Seed planting
1022	Magic tricks
1028	Drawing to music
1029	Masks
1033	Cotton candy, candy apples
1040	Pipe sculpture
1048	Book-making

Program #	Description of Activity
1049	Cake-making
1050	Cake-icing
1056	Pretend party
1059	Egg beater and detergent bubbles
1065	Storytelling (with hands and feet)
1070	Spoon-and-cup creations
1077	Shoe-box creations
1083	Drawing to music
1087	Paper chain
1089	Raspberry delight
1093	Clay sculpture
1095	Window cakes
1097	Lightbulb contraption
1099	Doughnuts
1105	Drawing to music
1106	Suitcase play
1107	Suitcase-making
1108	Magic tricks
1111	Paperweights
1113	Spin-the-wheel game
1114	Leather craft
1115	Hand prints
1116	Paper crown
1122	Calendar
1128	Paste and clay figure
1130	Orange juice
1131	Construction paper creations
1132	Puppet-making (papier-mâché)
1133	Popsicle-stick and modeling-dough creations
1136	Liquid experiment
1137	Collage
1140	Dancing out feelings
1144	Paintings
1145	Model airplane
1149	Upside-down cakes
1150	Comparison game
1152	Tool board
1154	Drawing to music

Program #	Description of Activity
1155	Go-cart
1156	Bead stringing
1163	Occupational signs
1166	Peanut butter
1172	Puppet-making
1173	Marble game
1174	Pepper experiment
1175	Fancy writing
1179	Cake decorating
1180	Newspaper hats
1184	Feel with eyes; rubbings
1185	Drawing to music
1188	Parent portraits
1189	Ice cream
1193	Box trolley
1194	Which-is-missing game
1195	Egg-decorating
1196	Paper bird
1197	Secret drawing; "OB" language
1198	Rubber-band ball
1204	Paddlewheel boat
1205	Toy box
1213	Musical instruments
1216	Magic tricks
1218	Follow-the-dot game
1220	Sand picture
1230	Leaf rubbings
1239	Tags
1240	Painting (drop-and splash)
1243	Ladder game
1244	Ice-cube and heater experiment
1248	Platanos fritos recipe
1251	Story-making
1253	Kaleidoscope picture
1255	Colored-water experiment
1262	Paper-cutting
1263	String design
1267	Hat-making

Program #	Description of Activity
1269	Music rhythms
1270	Sponge-painting
1276	Purple Cow recipe
1277	Puppet-making
1278	Box-making; take-it-away game
1280	Felt-board designs
1282	Panda toy
1283	Table-making; measuring
1284	Sundaes and sodas
1285	Chopsticks; paper bird
1286	Airplane; hangar
1287	Model airplane
1289	Sound comparisons
1291	Paper dolls
1292	Arm-and-hand exercises; painting
1294	Flashlight and lightning comparison
1295	Take-away game
1297	Dental examination; toothbrushing
1298	Animal sounds
1299	Potato plants
1301	Sound comparisons; cardboard box
1302	Library visit
1303	Music: loud and soft; open-and-closed eyes game
1305	Orange and grapefruit juice; which-is-which game
1306	Where-is-it game; flower parts; days of the week
1307	Tickets and vehicles; suitcase-packing
1308	Watering-can game; pull toy
1309	Masks
1310	Wax leaves
1311	Welcome-home sign
1312	Ukelele-tuning; stringed instruments; self-portrait
1313	Perception game; sound-making
1314	Chick hatching
1315	Vegetable prints; drum language
1316	Wallpaper-hanging
1317	Wallpaper-scrap game; complete-the-sequence game; greeting cards
1318	Pencil sharpener; pulley; winch

Program #	Description of Activity
1319	String-web plaque
1320	Gongs
1321	Book-making
1322	Book-making
1323	Pin-the-Star-on-the-Donkey game
1325	Bean bag and ring toss; music box; numbers
1326	Masking-tape designs
1327	Masking-tape designs
1328	Pizza-making
1330	Wall hanging; cardboard-tube game
1331	Clown-hanging
1332	Balloon animals
1334	Puppet-making; shadow box
1338	Which-is-which game; sandpainting; health drink; pine-apple plant
1340	"Tag" story
1342	Plaster castings
1344	Dot painting; Anniversary Delight recipe; numbers and Roman numerals
1345	Snowman
1346	Paper-cup game; coin trick
1347	Exercises
1348	Songwriting; leg exercises
1349	Bead-stringing
1350	Paper slippers
1351	Waterfall (with hands)
1352	On-and-off sign
1353	Family projects; spoon-and-ball game
1354	Spaghetti Marco Polo
1356	Perception game
1358	String ring
1359	Rhythm comparisons
1360	Spanish expressions
1361	Waffles; full-and-empty demonstration
1363	Paper-punch designs; Indian friendship dance
1364	Bottle organ
1365	Tower building; rock garden (miniature)
1367	Sound comparisons; washboard music; comb kazoo

Program #	Description of Activity
1368	Camera
1369	Jigsaw puzzle
1371	Doughnuts; lip-reading
1372	Mime
1373	Ukrainian Easter eggs; exercises
1374	Vibrations; facial expressions
1376	"Whole" and "part"
1377	Cup-building; blender drink
1379	Cardboard tube play; table-setting; weaving
1381	"Same" and "different"; player piano
1382	Toy house
1383	Painted-apple/real-apple comparison
1385	Bed tray; diorama; banana-fruit split
1386	Silk screening
1388	Puppet play; puppet stage
1389	Shoe-shining
1390	Icebox cake
1391	Hide-and-seek game; Frisbee toss
1392	Sandwiches; tap dancing
1393	Seat belts; size comparisons
1394	Inkblots
1395	Newspaper hat
1397	Block play
1398	Magnets; wood sculpture; horseshoe toss
1400	Burlap creations
1402	Placemat; foam-rubber flowers
1403	Terrariums
1404	Peek-a-boo game; noodle pudding
1405	Exercises; fingerpainting
1407	Juggling
1408	Modeling-dough recipe; wire and clay creations
1416	Tooth-flossing
1417	Sound comparisons
1418	Electrical appliances
1420	Recorder-playing; drawing to music
1422	Which-is-which game
1423	Taffy; fingerpainting
1426	Ballet

Program #	Description of Activity
1427	Model glider
1430	Baton twirling
1431	Jigsaw puzzle
1433	Tacos
1435	Rubbings
1441	Stained-glass window
1443	Wax-paper-and-comb instrument
1445	Watermelon boats; fruit comparisons
1446	Indian dancing
1447	Exercises
1448	Paper basket
1449	Bean bags; bean-bag games
1452	Modeling-dough creation
1453	Witch's hat
1455	Bread-making
1459	Collage; glitter picture
1462	Counting
1467	"Vegetreat" creation
1468	Clay dinosaur; block house
1470	Tapioca pudding
1471	Organ sounds
1472	Knitting machine
1473	Banana breads
1474	Weather station
1476	Paper-cup building
1477	Pretzels
1478	Block garage
1480	Clown mask
1481	Seat construction
1482	Art gallery visit
1485	Rainbow-making
1486	Ventriloquism
1487	Block structure
1488	Make-believe toys
1490	Stilts
1491	Piano roll; cheese and banana treat
1492	Pellet picture
1493	Cookie-making; toy clarinet

Program #	Description of Activity
1494	Ice skating
1495	Favorite objects
1496	Stuffed animals
1497	Instant camera
1500	Zoo visit
1501	Spoon-playing
1502	Trees; emergency room
1503	Seat belts
1504	Horns
1507	Bubble-making
1508	Cheese sandwich
1509	Bottle flute
1510	Rope-and-pulley magic
1511	Towels
1512	Block play; paper game
1513	Robot
1514	Hopscotch
1515	Board game; harmonica
1516	Rug-making
1519	Wearing glasses
1520	Graham crackers
1521	Shape game
1523	Marimba and drums
1524	Bridge-building
1526	Rainbow-making
1527	Milk-carton blocks
1530	Chalk art
1531	Cardboard trolley
1532	Wind chimes
1537	Granola and raisin recipe
1538	Peanut butter and banana recipe
1539	Vegetables
1540	Spaghetti
1544	Rice treats
1545	Clay bowl
1548	Hand-clapping
1549	Paper hat; tube instrument
1550	Piano play

MISTER ROGERS' PLAYBOOK ACTIVITIES INDEX

244   ACTIVITIES INDEX

SUBJECT INDEX

Chef Brockett's nutritious snack, *(212)*
Clapping, *(126-127)*
Collections, boxes for, *(48)*
Colors, favorite, *(123)*
Competition, *(75)*
Coping, play and, *(35-37)*
Crayons, *(113)*
Creativity, *(6-8, 230)*
Crises, coping with, *(35-37)*
Curiosity of part and counterpart, *(18-19)*

Death, *(148)*
Difference-similarity exploration. *See* Similarity-difference exploration
Discovery, *see* Exploration
Drawing(s)
    outline of body, *(45-46)*
    sand, *(134-135)*
    of self, *(47)*
    See also Art projects

Emotions
    aggressive, *(27-28)*
    expression of, *(36)*
    pretending and, *(82)*
"Everything Grows Together" (song), *(52-53)*
Exercises, 52-66
    inside, *(62-66)*
    outside, *(52-62)*
Exploration, *(111-143)*
    of differences and similarities, *(117-125)*
    of buttons, *(119-120)*
    of colors, *(123)*
    of families, *(123)*
    of keys, *(121-122)*
    of laundry colors, *(120-121)*
    of lotto cards, *(123-125)*
    of partially-hidden objects, *(122)*

of people, *(122-123)*
of rough and smooth, *(121)*
of musical designs, *(131)*
of musical instruments, *(126-131)*
    bass fiddles, *(129)*
    blocks, *(129)*
    cardboard horns, *(127)*
    chimes, *(128)*
    clapping and, *(126-127)*
    drums, *(128)*
    gongs, *(130-131)*
    guitarlike instruments and, *(127-128)*
    maracas, *(129)*
    tapping cheeks and, *(127)*
    voice and, *(127)*
    water-filled glasses, *(130)*
with rubbings, *(114-115)*
with senses, *(111-112)*
of shapes and colors, *(113-114, 131-134)*
of sounds, *(115-117)*

Fairness, play and, *(107-108)*
Fears of children, respecting, *(22-23)*
Feelings
    aggressive, *(27-28)*
    expression of, *(36)*
    pretending and, *(82)*
Finger painting, *(19-20, 47)*
Food recipes, *(211-216)*
    banana boat, *(211)*
    Chef Brockett's nutritious snack, *(212)*
    granola, *(212-213)*
    José's *arroz con leche* (rice with milk), *(212)*
    noodle pudding, *(213)*
    platanos fritos (fried bananas), *(213)*
    soft pretzels, *(213-214)*
    spaghetti Marco Polo, *(214-215)*
    tofu burgers, *(215)*

foot, *(47)*

string, *(131-132)*

See also Art projects

Parents' patience, play and, *(15-16)*

Peek-a-boo games, *(162-164)*

with paper windows, *(67-69)*

Pictures

invisible, *(134)*

on sticks, *(92-93)*

Pillowcases

dyed, *(50)*

stuffed, *(48-50)*

Platanos fritos, (213)

Play, *(3-11)*

adults' vs. children's, *(3-4)*

authority and, *(141-143)*

beginning of, *(4-5)*

cause-effect relationships and, *(175-176)*

coping and, *(35-37)*

creativity and, *(6-8, 230)*

defining, *(3)*

expression of emotions through, *(36)*

fairness and, *(107-108)*

imitation and, *(6)*

independence and, *(73-75)*

mother-infant, *(5)*

parents' patience and, *(15-16)*

phases of, *(16-17)*

self-concept and, *(5, 6)*

sense of safety and, *(23)*

as serious learning, *(229-230)*

Pretending, *(79-104)*

with crowns, *(101-102)*

with false beards, *(100-101)*

with false moustache, *(101)*

feelings and, *(82)*

with hats, *(102-103)*

importance of, *(83)*

with masks, *(100)*

with slippers, *(103-104)*

See also Journeys, pretend;
Puppets

Pretzels, soft, *(213-214)*

Problem-solving, *(7)*

Pudding, noodle, *(213)*

Puppets, *(83-89)*

box, *(97)*

making, *(87-100)*

marionettes, *(98-99)*

paper-bag, *(97)*

sock, *(98)*

spoon, *(88-91)*

stage for, *(83-87)*

stick, *(91-96)*

Puzzles, *(25)*

Remembering, *(112)*

Rhymes, nonsense, *(167-169)*

Rice with milk, *(212)*

Roughness-softness difference, *(121)*

Safety, sense of, *(23)*

Self, drawings of, *(47)*

Self-concept, *(45-51)*

play and, *(5, 6)*

Self-control, *(62)*

Self-expression, *(6)*

Senses, *(111-112)*

Separation anxiety, *(148-149)*

toddlers' activities and, *(23-25)*

See also Journeys, pretend

Similarity-difference exploration, *(117-125)*

of buttons, *(119-120)*

of colors, *(123)*

of families, *(123)*

of keys, *(121-122)*

of laundry colors, *(120-121)*

of lotto cards, *(123-125)*

of partially-hidden objects, *(122)*

of people, *(122-123)*

of surfaces, *(121)*

Snacks, *(212)*

Softness-roughness difference, *(121)*

Softing games, *(26-27)*

with cards, *(123)*

with keys, *(121-122)*
with laundry, *(120-121)*
Sounds, exploration of, *(115-117)*
Spaghetti Marco Polo, *(214-215)*
Stage, puppet, *(83-87)*
Sticks, pictures on, *(92-93)*

Tasting, *(111-112)*
Teething, *(21)*
Toddlers' activities
 awareness of size differences
 and, *(18)*
 biting urge and, *(20)*
 identity formation and, *(25-28)*
 ins and outs of objects and, *(17)*
 messiness and, *(19-20)*
 part and counterpart curiosity
 and, *(18-19)*
 preoccupation with mouth and,
 (21-23)
 separation anxiety and, *(23-25)*

Tofu
 burgers, *(215)*
 with onions and cheese sauce,
 (211)
Trumpet, ear, *(116-117)*
Two-year-olds. *See* Toddlers'
 activities

Upsets, kinds of, *(36)*

Vegetable burgers, *(215-216)*

"Wiggle-waggle" (finger game),
 (59)
Wishing, *(82-83)*

Zoo, model of, *(203-210)*
 animals for, *(207-210)*
 cages for, *(204-207)*

STARTING TODAY, WE ARE TO SERVE AS YOUR PERSONAL GUARD, MY LADY.

I AM SEYMORE OF THE IMPERIAL GUARD.

I AM JUNE. BY YOUR LEAVE, MY LADY.

UH, YES...

LIKEWISE, I'LL BE IN YOUR HANDS.

TO THINK THEY'D REALLY SEND NOT JUST ONE, BUT TWO IMPERIAL GUARDSMEN...